Playing for Rangers No 11

PLAYING FOR RANGERS NO 11

Edited by Ken Gallacher

Stanley Paul, London

Stanley Paul & Co. Ltd
3 Fitzroy Square, London W1P 6JD

An imprint of the Hutchinson Publishing Group

London Melbourne Sydney Auckland
Wellington Johannesburg and agencies
throughout the world

First published 1979
©Stanley Paul & Co. Ltd 1979

Set in VIP Baskerville by N.G. Graphics Ltd.
Printed in Great Britain by The Anchor Press Ltd
and bound by Wm Brendon & Son Ltd
both of Tiptree, Essex

ISBN 0 09 139301 9

Black and white photographs by Sportapics
Colour photographs of Bobby Russell in the Cup
Final, Rangers scoring v Celtic, the League Cup
Final, Rangers v Cologne by Sportapics; all
others by Colorsport

Frontispiece:
Rangers' goalkeeper leaps in the air to foil Killie striker John Bourke, one
of the Rugby Park team's danger men. Colin Jackson is grounded while
Tom Forsyth looks on

CONTENTS

Early in the season Ally Dawson had to duel for the left back spot with
Manchester United's Alex Forsyth who was on loan to Rangers. Here
Forsyth moves in to tackle Celtic's winger Dave Provan in an Old Firm
clash

THE START OF A NEW ERA

When John Greig took over as manager of Rangers in the summer of 1978 there was a promise of change in the air.

Not a change in personnel — though Greig did bid for two new players — but a change in style. Greig, the strong man defender for so many years, wanted a different approach from the team he was taking over. He wanted to build a side which would play football from the back. He wanted to see everyone in the team try to play with style. Greig emphasized that he didn't want to see long clearances booted upfield for forwards to chase. Instead he looked for a more skilful, more patient build-up. In short he wanted a European look about his team.

He succeeded in getting the change he wanted. As well as being a team of winners the Ibrox men also became a team of style. When they marched into Europe, they did so with a modern look about their play. Instead of the old-fashioned cavalry charges which had failed so often in the past there was a sophistication about their play which impressed those so-defensive men of Juventus the Italian champions, and the skilled and subtle Dutchmen of PSV Eindhoven.

These victories were the landmarks of the early part of the season. They proved to everyone that Rangers could compete with the best the Continent had to offer while getting on with their own job at home.

They were important for Greig, too. His tactics worked superbly in both games and the players who had played along-side him for so many seasons, knew that he had taken the step upstairs to the manager's office successfully.

It was important that the new era, the Greig era, began with success. And that proved to be more difficult to come by than the change of style had been . . . .

After long, hard battles Rangers fought back to win the League Cup against Aberdeen in the Hampden final which at one point they looked like losing. It was the first honour . . . and another was to follow.

The second trophy for Greig's Rangers was the Scottish Cup and no team in the history of the competition has had to fight so hard to win that honour. Twice in the earlier rounds Rangers were forced into replays, against Kilmarnock and then against Partick Thistle, before they won through. Then it was on to that epic clash with Hibs in the final.

Three times the teams met before they could be separated. The first final ended in a 0-0 draw. The second, plus extra time, finished the same way. Then it was on to clash number three and a final which was unforgettable. Once again the game was forced into extra time before Rangers finally clinched the Cup with a 3-2 win after five and a half hours of football.

But the Cup was won and it joined the League Cup in the glittering trophy room at Ibrox. So the Greig era has begun with success and with style, and much more of both will follow as John Greig manages the club he played for with such distinction for eighteen years!

MY FIRST YEAR AS BOSS
by John Greig

The transition from player to manager is a difficult one . . .
even more difficult when you make the change while remaining with the same club. It has been done successfully, but not
too often.

Typically John Greig, for so long Rangers' captain, accepted
that challenge when he was appointed Ibrox team boss and
brought Rangers the success they demand. Here the Rangers
manager answers questions on his first year — a year which
brought the Scottish Cup and League Cup to Ibrox. The
questions were put by editor Ken Gallacher . . . .

GALLACHER — It is always difficult to move directly from
the playing staff into the manager's office, for a variety of
reasons. But I would have thought it was still harder for you.
The season before you took over the club had won the 'treble'
and you, as a new boy in a managerial sense, had to follow that
achievement. How hard was that to do?

GREIG — It was hard. There is no use saying otherwise. But
I'd been with Rangers as a player for eighteen years and I'd
been the team captain for most of that time. That meant the
supporters were ready to be patient with me. The fans told me
that themselves. They would not have liked it if the team had
won nothing — I wouldn't have liked it very much either —
but they would have given me time to settle into the job.

As for the other aspect — well, the players made it easy for
me. From the first day I sat down in the manager's office they
called me 'Boss'. That's from the youngest players on the staff
to the oldest, from all the lads I'd been playing with down
through the years, I was given instant respect.

I would have asked them for that, but I didn't have to. They
gave it to me and it was important. During the season we had
our differences, our rows if you like. But that was a good thing.
I welcomed them because it helped spell out that I wasn't the
joker in the dressing-room any more. I wasn't one of the lads
— I was the manager. I was the man they had to discuss

contracts with, the man who had to discipline them if they stepped out of line, the man who was in charge of the team. To be fair to them they accepted that marvellously.

GALLACHER — In fact you ended the season by retaining two of three major trophies. Did that satisfy you in your first season?

GREIG — In a way it did. If someone had said to me when I was a player that I would become manager and win two trophies in my first season I would have settled for that. But last season was different. I was bitterly disappointed that we did not win the 'treble' again. We could have done it and we failed.

Maybe it sounds greedy but I wanted the 'treble' last year and that will be my aim every year. I still believe that we were the best team in the country last year and that's why we should have lifted all three trophies. Still, it wasn't to be. But I'll go on aiming for that at the start of the season. It is the way it has to be with Rangers. I think that I have the best job in the country because I am with the best club in the country. Therefore they have to have success.

GALLACHER — You had a taste of European success again last year and you had hoped for that. Did that please you?

GREIG — Of course it did. I took a lot of satisfaction from the victories over Juventus and PSV Eindhoven. It ended disappointingly against Cologne but we had a pile of commitments by the time we met them because of the extraordinary season we had suffered. So many games, important games, loomed at the same time. The League Cup Final was at the end of March when it should have been finished before Christmas . . . so we were involved in four tournaments around that time. The European Cup, the League Championship, the League Cup and the Scottish Cup. It was a lot.

But, basically, I wanted to re-build our reputation a little in Europe. I wanted Rangers' name to be respected — feared if you like — once more.

The two really good results we had, and the fact that we lost by just the odd goal to Cologne in the quarter finals, will have given us that. I'm sure that in the Cup Winners' Cup next season any team drawn against us will not relish the thought of coming to Ibrox to play.

I suppose the Juventus result gave me most satisfaction of all. I'd come up against Italian teams so often, for Rangers and Scotland, and finished up being beaten. Sometimes we might

10

The first view the public had of John Greig in his new role as manager — in the team group taken before the start of the season. After eighteen years in a strip, Greig joins the squad here in a suit for the first time. He managed to retain two of the three trophies they had when they started the season

have played well enough, might have attacked them well enough, but we'd still lose. And I'd be left wondering what we had to do against them. This time, drawing Juventus with all those World Cup men from the Italian national team, it seemed as if we didn't have any chance at all. But we won and we won well and tactically I felt that I had learned a lot from that match.

GALLACHER — It was a battle of wits, of course, wasn't it?
GREIG — Very much so. I relished that, though. I'd often felt that we went into these games without enough preparation. We just got our heads down and charged at teams and we lost out to them. One reason was that we tried to play two games, one in Europe and one at home and the mix didn't always

Derek Johnstone, Greig's choice as the captain to succeed himself,
battles in the air with Celtic centre half Roddie MacDonald

work. That's why I tried to get the team playing football from the back when I took over. I wanted to build a team style which would work in Europe — but which could also bring success at home.

GALLACHER — How did the players react to that?
GREIG — There were a few teething problems but I think the results speak for themselves. I think they looked on it as a challenge. They picked up the challenge and I thought there were times during the season when we played magnificent football.

GALLACHER — I suppose that with Rangers you have to aim for European success as well as domestic success.
GREIG — Yes, but the domestic success is the first priority. We want to win one of the major honours at home and be certain of being in Europe every season. That has to be the first aim.

GALLACHER — Yes, admittedly, but the club's horizons are not limited to that, are they?
GREIG — Of course not. This is an ambitious club. We have won the European Cup Winners' Cup once and been beaten finalists twice. We want that kind of performance regularly. For a few seasons we fell in the early stages before the younger players could pick up the kind of experience which is vital to them. You can't buy the experience that players like Colin Jackson, Alex MacDonald, Tommy McLean, Sandy Jardine and Derek Johnstone have. These are players who have come through long European campaigns and now I want to give the younger members of the team the chance to pick up that kind of European training. You can only get it by playing in top level games on the Continent.

So, that is a target for us, too. But we have to be the best team in Scotland. That has to be a constant aim for this club. The supporters don't want anything less from us.

GALLACHER — The way you say that makes it sound as if you have a permanently difficult job on your hands . . . a job which demands so much success from you and the players?
GREIG — I suppose you could say that — but I enjoy it. It was always in my mind that I'd like to be a manager and obviously having played with Rangers for so long it was tremendous to get this chance. I love every minute of it. OK, it's hard. I think I had about four days off in the whole season but the rewards were there. The League Cup came first and then the Scottish Cup followed and it's great to be a part of that kind of success.

Veteran centre half Colin Jackson has just cleared here from St Mirren striker Frank McGarvey, since sold to Liverpool. Greig says Jackson was his most consistent player in the last months of the season

GALLACHER — You kept a very low profile during the season. Why was that?

GREIG — Because I'm still a learner at the job. I'm trying to learn all the time. I didn't look for any publicity and I didn't go on the telly or anything because I had enough to do sitting behind this manager's desk. Mind you, I was very lucky that Willie Waddell and Willie Thornton were on hand. I could turn to them for advice and they have something like eighty years of experience in the game between the two of them. It's marvellous to be able to fall back on them for support.

Then I had my coach Joe Mason, Stan Anderson who came back to run the reserves, and Tom Craig the physiotherapist all in the backroom so to speak. But, mostly, I had my players. Anything accomplished was accomplished by them.

GALLACHER — Is that why you stayed out of sight when the team won the Scottish Cup Final against Hibs, even though the Rangers fans were chanting your name?

GREIG — Yes it was. I have had my time on the field. I've held up Cups and I've gone on laps of honour and it was great. But

Little Tommy McLean — his kind of European experience has been vital, says the new Rangers boss

it's over for me now. It's to do with Derek Johnstone, who is captain now, and all the other players. It was their night and I didn't want to take anything away from them.

My job is done off the field and I'm happy to stay there. Mind you, I'm like everyone else. It was tremendous to hear the supporters chanting for me. I enjoyed that — I just hope they go on doing it. But, at the same time, the game is about players and when they have won a trophy then I believe they should celebrate it without me.

GALLACHER — Did it worry you that you might not win a trophy in your first season?

GREIG — It did a little bit because I remember the dark days when I took over as captain and I went a long, long time without winning anything. I didn't want that to happen to me as a manager or to Derek Johnstone as a captain. They weren't good days and I don't want to think of them coming back.

GALLACHER — Talking about players, I know you have youngsters you are looking to break through, but you also have older players, quite a few around the thirty mark. Does this concern you?

GREIG — I don't know how I can answer that one properly. It isn't for me to judge when a player should pack up. I went on to a fair age myself so how can I tell someone else he is too old? It is different with each individual player. Look at Colin Jackson who is the oldest player in the current team and tell me if there was anyone better in the last few months of the season. He played superbly so how can you suggest when anyone's career is over?

I do have some good youngsters, some really good players, almost ready to break through into the League team. Two of them were in the dug out with me at the Scottish Cup Final, Steve Richardson and John MacDonald. I wanted them there to get the feel of the big occasion. OK, they are both just sixteen years of age but they will benefit from just having been in that atmosphere.

GALLACHER — Is the future of the club with youngsters like these or with buying good solid experienced players?

GREIG — It's hard to say one way or the other. Possibly it could be a bit of both. If someone I think would benefit this club comes onto the transfer market then I would bid for him. But it would have to be a player who would strengthen the squad. He might not go straight into the first team, but if he was an asset to the pool of players I have then I would buy him. There is money available if I want to buy players. I made a bid of £250,000 at the start of last season for two players, Brian Whittaker and Gregor Stevens. We didn't get them but if I want money for players then I will get the money. But the youngsters are vital to the long term development of Rangers and we do have good youngsters!

Manager John Greig emphasizes a point to Gordon Smith as the players relax before extra time in the Scottish Cup Final second replay with Hibs

At the end of the season I went with our youth team to Croix in France. We won the tournament, were awarded a trophy for being the most attractive team in the tournament, won another trophy for scoring the most goals and John MacDonald was named the outstanding player in the tournament. I was delighted.

GALLACHER — But you wouldn't hesitate to spend if you felt you had to?
GREIG — No. The bid I made for the two lads last season shows that. The board have told me that there is money there if I want it. But I won't spend for spending's sake.

GALLACHER — Finally, what has given you most satisfaction after the first year as manager?
GREIG — Well, I've talked about many of the things which have pleased me. The way the players accepted me . . . winning the two trophies . . . doing quite well in Europe . . . all of these things gave me satisfaction. But, personally, I got a great deal of satisfaction out of the fact that I was able to repay the directors for giving me the job. It was a bold decision by them to give the Rangers manager's job to someone who had no managerial experience. They did it and I just hope that winning the Scottish Cup and the League Cup repaid them a little for the faith they had in me.

Now all I want is to give them back that Premier League title next year . . . .

17

JOY AGAINST JUVENTUS

Rangers' new boss John Greig had scarcely settled into the manager's office at Ibrox when he was pitched into one of the toughest European tests the Scottish champions had ever faced.

The first round draw for the European Champions' Cup paired Rangers with the pride of Italy, Juventus. The Turin-based team boasted nine of the players who had been in the Italian World Cup squad in Argentina — a squad which had found success there, and one which was respected across the world. Not just in Europe!

This, then, was the first great task Greig had to face. He set about it with the thoroughness which was to become a hall-mark of his progress in Europe. A week-end dash to Milan allowed him to see Juventus play AC Milan in a pre-season tournament. The Milan team won 4-2 and Greig returned feeling more heartened than at any time since the draw was made. He admitted cautiously: 'I saw a couple of problems and their goalkeeper Dino Zoff might be a worry for them. He was to blame for two of the goals . . . and he has been under pressure from the fans because they blame him for their team not winning the World Cup.'

There were other points, too, that Greig picked up on. In particular he noticed that the Italians — like most teams from that rigidly-disciplined football country — stuck to a fairly stereotyped style of play. That gave him ideas . . .

Yet he knew, too, that Juventus with all their stars and all their experience, could not be underestimated. Two years earlier Juventus had won the UEFA Cup and on the way to that triumph had beaten Manchester City and Manchester United.

City's Scottish midfield star Asa Hartford told me before the Rangers clash: 'They will try to intimidate Rangers when they play in Turin. That is a certainty.

'They will test Rangers over there and try to get them involved. They are a highly-skilled team — with men such as

18

Three of the star-studded Italian defence are outjumped here by Rangers' centre half Colin Jackson as the Scots head towards their Ibrox European Cup victory over Juventus

Bettega, Tardelli and Causio they must be! But they will still have a little go just to upset the Rangers lads. The team hasn't changed much since we played them. The new left back from Argentina, Cabrini, is in and the centre who cost them one and a half million pounds has replaced Boninsegna — these aren't changes to weaken them any.

'But Rangers will have an advantage from playing the first leg away from home. No matter how good any Italian team may be they don't score a lot of goals. So when they have to play at home first they are under pressure to build up a good lead. They don't like that situation at all. But away from home they will tie things up. We could get only one goal at Maine

Road, United got one at Old Trafford — and it wasn't enough for either of us!'

Greig knew that his opposite number Giovanni Trappatoni, coach of Juventus and one time midfield ace with AC Milan and Italy, was uncomfortable at the thought of playing at home first. He also knew that Trappatoni and his players expected the Scottish champions to be no more than a stepping stone towards the next round and towards a possible European Cup win.

The Italians were entitled to hold that view. Rangers' European form over a number of years had been poor, although Greig was determined to alter that fading image. Just as Greig had watched Juventus, so did Trappatoni look at Rangers, in a drawn game with Hibs at Easter Road and then in the defeat by Celtic at Parkhead. He made polite noises, admired some of Rangers' players, including Alex MacDonald and Gordon Smith, and jetted back to Italy believing his team would march into the second round confidently.

Most people thought the same but Greig, in spite of his team's poor League opening, clung doggedly to the belief that Europe would lift them back to their true form. As the players settled into the luxury surroundings of the exclusive Villa Sassi on the outskirts of Turin before the game, the young Rangers boss maintained: 'The names of the men they have to face will inspire my players. We will play it tight, we must do that because to achieve success in Europe you have to be disciplined in defence.

'We have to be patient, we have to use all our experience and we cannot approach the game the way we approach games at home. This is a different kind of football . . . .'

Greig could not name his own team on the eve of the clash in the Stadio Communale. A mystery injury held up his choice and he was not unhappy at that. He wanted to keep Trappatoni guessing a little longer about the Ibrox line up and about their tactical intentions. What he did do, however, was name the team he expected Juventus to field. And a couple of hours later Trappatoni announced exactly the eleven men Greig expected. Eight of the World Cup men were in — Dino Zoff in goal, Antonello Cuccureddu and Antonio Cabrini at full back, Gaetano Scirea as 'sweeper', Marco Tardelli and Romeo Benetti in midfield and Franco Causio and Roberta Bettega up front. The other three places went to Francesco Morini at centre half, Guiseppe Furino in midfield and Pietro Virdis as striker. It was a team which would have struck fear into any side in the world. And with sixty thousand people

It's Rangers' first goal at Ibrox against the Italian champions in the European Cup clash. Little Alex MacDonald thrusts forward to head the ball in with goalkeeper Dino Zoff stranded behind him. Striker Roberto Bettega chases back helplessly. The other Rangers player is Gordon Smith

backing them in their own Stadium the following night it was hard to imagine Rangers, so often found out in Europe, surviving to the second round.

Black and white banners fluttered in the night sky, rockets exploded over the concrete bowl of the Stadio Communale and the thousand or so Rangers supporters found it difficult to cheer their heroes in the torrid atmosphere as the teams took the field for that crucial first leg match.

Greig's team had been named and it was: McCloy; Jardine, A. Forsyth; T. Forsyth, Jackson, MacDonald, Miller, Russell, Parlane, Smith, Watson. Wingers Tommy McLean and Davie Cooper were on the bench as Greig made it plain that this was to be a holding exercise . . . one which would leave Rangers in the driving seat when the second leg was played at Ibrox two weeks later. That was what he hoped for, what he planned for

Not this time, Bobby! As Rangers' midfield man Bobby Russell tries to get through he is tackled by Italian defender Gaetano Scirea in the second leg of the European Cup game

and yet, before Rangers had adjusted to their new tactical set up they had gone a goal behind after just eight minutes. Pietro Virdis was the man who scored, escaping from Jackson to hook a shot into the net.

Agony was etched on Greig's face as he left the dug out to shout advice to his players. He had wanted to avoid giving away an early goal . . . now the Italians surged forward in great attacking waves.

It was then, though, as the rockets and fire crackers were still exploding, as the Italians urged their team on towards a famous victory, that the discipline Greig had emphasized so strongly before the game became evident. The players settled to their jobs . . . Alex Miller began to curb the forward dashes of Cabrini; Colin Jackson and Tom Forsyth picked up the twin strikers, Virdis and Bettega; Alex Forsyth stuck grimly to the explosive Causio and up front, often on his own, Derek Parlane chased and harried and fought for the few balls which came his way. Gradually the attacks began to lose their momentum, gradually the Rangers support began to be heard from the corner of the stadium they had occupied. Gradually, in fact, Rangers began to edge forward themselves. Nervously to begin with, yet with growing assurance as the minutes ticked away and the pressure moved onto the Italians. Parlane had one shot scrambled away by Zoff and then the keeper held a free kick from Kenny Watson.

Just once more before half time Rangers came close to cracking. Cabrini broke clear of the determined Miller and crossed low. Sandy Jardine, playing so efficiently as 'sweeper' behind the defence, slid in to clear and played the ball against the post. It was a let off!

In the second half Juventus began to run out of ideas and it was the dying minutes before McCloy was needed. And how magnificently he responded to the call, rising to turn a header from Bettega over the bar. Earlier the ugly side of Italian football had been shown by the Juventus hatchet man, Romeo Benetti. The man whose foul on Kevin Keegan at Wembley had shocked everyone, scythed down Gordon Smith.He had been booked in the first half along with Tom Forsyth and this time should have been ordered off. But the Rumanian referee took no action. It was left to Trappatoni to take Benetti off and push on Fanna as substitute.

It was, however, the single unsavoury incident in the game and Greig admitted later: 'It might have turned out worse if Trappatoni had not acted so quickly. I admire the way he did that. But I admire the way my players reacted more than anything else. They showed more discipline than any other Rangers team I've been connected with. I could not have asked for more from them. The way they recovered after losing that early goal was magnificent. Now it's on to Ibrox and we have a psychological advantage now . . . I'm sure of that!'

Greig was correct once more. The advantage had gone to Rangers because Trappatoni had failed to get the two goal lead he was certain he would need in Glasgow. Yet, also, Rangers' performance, so professional, so accomplished tactically, had rung warning bells among the Italians. They knew they were going to face a team which had already out-thought them — and they were determined that would not be

An action study of the one million pound striker from Juventus, Pietro Virdis, who scored against Rangers in Turin

allowed to happen again. But, two weeks later, in front of a 44,000 capacity Ibrox crowd, it did . . . .

Once more Greig kept the Italians guessing about his team. He knew he had Derek Johnstone available again after missing the first leg through a UEFA suspension, just as he knew that Claudio Gentile, another of the Italian World Cup squad, was available for Juventus also after being suspended.

The current strength of Juventus had been underlined by Italy the previous week when seven of the team had played against Bulgaria and then five had been used against Turkey in another friendly. Roberto Bettega had not played against Turkey because of injury — but he was fit for Ibrox. Greig had expected that. The one surprise was that bad boy Benetti was relegated to a place on the bench to allow Gentile to play.

Greig took his players to Largs and instilled into them there that patience was required again. 'We cannot go charging into attack looking for goals and leave ourselves short at the back,' he emphasized. 'Against a team like this, bred on counter-attacking, it would be fatal. We shall look for the goals but with

24

patience and I have a couple of things to try out against them. We might just catch them out.'

Greig's side for the return was: McCloy; Jardine, A. Forsyth; T. Forsyth, Jackson, MacDonald; McLean, Russell, Parlane, Johnstone, Smith. The Italians made just the solitary change, Gentile taking Benetti's place.

Yet, in spite of the optimism, the spectre of poor Premier League displays still hung over Rangers. They had still to score a win in their own domestic League competition. How could they expect to beat the star-studded champions of Italy, asked the still-confident Italian journalists.

In 17 minutes they received their answer. Little Tommy McLean had drifted to the left and caused some consternation in the man-for-man marking system used by the Italian defence. While that confusion lasted Rangers struck. Predictably it was the tiny McLean who started it with a neat pass to Bobby Russell from a free kick.

On the ball went to the over-lapping Alex Forsyth. He shot. It was blocked. Gordon Smith got to it, sent it for goal and the veteran Zoff could only push it out. There was Alex MacDonald surging through to ram a header into the net.

The Italians were worried after that as Rangers dominated play and dictated the direction of the match. And in 68 minutes Rangers scored that vital second goal. Bobby Russell

It's European Cup joy for Rangers as their number 11, Gordon Smith, sends in the winning goal against Juventus whose World Cup goalkeeper Dino Zoff sprawls helplessly along his line

swung a free kick into goal, the Italians misjudged it and Gordon Smith rose to send a header soaring beyond Zoff.

The Italians knew that just one goal was needed for them still to take the tie on the away goals counting double rule. On came Benetti and Fanna to replace Furino and Tardelli . . . but while they did attack a little more, Rangers were able to master their forward flurries. It was left to Benetti with another foul on Smith to upset Rangers but by then the game was over and Rangers had beaten the Italians. They had also reasserted themselves as a force in Europe after five years in the wilderness.

That's what delighted John Greig so much after the game. 'All Europe will sit up and take notice of this result,' he grinned. 'As manager I wanted desperately to put us back in the European spotlight. This will have done it and we have to continue to do well in this tournament. The European Cup builds reputations on the Continent.

'This was practically the Italian World Cup team, remember. That kind of team would be feared anywhere in the world. No praise can be high enough for the Rangers players tonight. They completed the job they started in Turin — and they did it as professionally as any team could have done!'

While Greig heaped praise onto his players it was still difficult to belittle his own achievement. He had been able to out-think the Italians over the two games. He had also been able to get his team to play with the discipline necessary in Europe. For instance, he had had the courage to play with a 'sweeper' behind his defence at Ibrox in the second leg. Sandy Jardine had gone there to act as the safety net behind Tom Forsyth and Colin Jackson in case Bettega or Virdis slipped clear.

That was a far cry from the buccaneering days when Rangers pushed forward, hurling players into attacks, and then being hit by swift and lethal sucker punches at the back. It had happened often before and the fans, so unwilling to show patience, had contributed to some of the crazy cavalry charge attacks which had meant Rangers' European downfall. The crowds are always magnificent in support but sometimes they have refused to accept that European football can be a cat-and-mouse game of tactics. This time they did.

Rangers were able to stick to the system laid down by Greig before the game and they notched one of the Ibrox club's most famous victories in Europe. Yet Greig would not allow himself or his players to be carried away by the joy of that one victory.

More action around that Juventus goal as Alex MacDonald, on the ground, watches a header sail for goal. Other Rangers men in the picture are Derek Johnstone and Colin Jackson, while the Italian defenders are Guiseppe Furino and Franco Causio

'Look,' he told me the day after the second leg game, 'that is a first round match. OK, it was the most powerful opposition we could face. They must have been near favourites to win and they were a tremendous team — but all we have done is get through to round two. We can't go shouting about European success yet. There is a bit to go.

'I just hope that the draw gives us another top club. I don't have any preferences but a top team brings out the best in us

Alex Forsyth, on loan from Manchester United, played a key role against Juventus, blotting out their World Cup ace Franco Causio in the two games. Here, though, he is seen taking the ball from another danger man, Frank McGarvey, then of St Mirren but now with Liverpool

and it also gives the players a chance to learn exactly what top class European football is all about. They will be better players after this tie against Juventus and I want that improvement to continue.'

The holders, Liverpool, had gone out, victims of Brian Clough's Nottingham Forest. The beaten finalists, Bruges, had been beaten by Wisla Cracow of Poland and Rangers had taken care of one of the other semi-finalists, Juventus, while the other team from the previous year's last four, Borussia Moenchengladbach had not qualified. The way seemed open for a team to make a name for themselves, or, like Rangers, to carve out a new reputation. Greig wanted a quality draw and the next day when it was made that is exactly what he got.

The jubilation among the supporters was suddenly muted. For, after Juventus, Rangers were paired with PSV Eindhoven, the Dutch champions who had six men from Holland's World Cup squad in their side. It was another awesome task . . . .

RANGERS WIN THEIR OWN TOURNAMENT – AT LAST!

There was one domestic trophy, just a little, local one, which John Greig had never been able to win in his days as a Rangers player. Twice he had captained Rangers teams competing for it and twice he had ended up on the losing side.

Which was why there was some importance attached to the pre-season Ibrox tournament last summer. Greig wanted to win the Tennent-Caledonian trophy and he wanted, too, to give the fans a preview of the kind of football he hoped to produce from his team in the season which loomed ahead. It was the third year of the competition and in the two previous tournaments the trophy had moved south, taken there first by Southampton and then by West Bromwich Albion . . . and these two teams were both taking part in the competition again along with newly-promoted Hearts.

Greig wanted things to change. Especially he wanted the trophy to remain at Ibrox, sitting alongside so many others in the trophy room. Yet, he knew, too, just how difficult it would be. He explained before the matches kicked off for the two day double-header programmes: 'It annoys me that we haven't been able to win this tournament, but this week-end we have to gain something which we can use in the new season. It would be fine to win but next Saturday when the League begins is the important time for us!

'West Brom won it last year and they went on to do magnificently in England last season. Southampton have won it and now they have been promoted, like Hearts, so they want to show that they deserve that promotion. It won't be easy . . . .'

Yet, for once, Greig was wrong. It turned out to be very much easier than anyone had expected. For Rangers struck the groove their new boss had hoped for. The draw had paired the two English teams together for the first round games and the two Scots teams together also. The winners met in the final with the other two playing off for third and fourth places — exactly the format which had been used so successfully in the previous two seasons.

Alex Forsyth, seen here about to tackle Paul Sturrock of Dundee United, made his Rangers debut in the Tennent-Caledonian Tournament and scored his first goal for the Ibrox club

With twenty-five thousand fans at Ibrox, Southampton and West Brom drew 1-1 and then Lawrie McMenemy's team won 4-1 on penalties to qualify for the final for the second time in three years. Even the support given to West Brom when ex-Ibrox favourite Willie Johnston appeared for them in the second half couldn't help. West Brom had led from a superb first half goal scored by Cyrille Regis and the game had only been saved for Saints by a Phil Boyer goal four minutes from the end. Then came the penalties . . . and it was Southampton who made certain with them.

Rangers didn't need penalties in their game against Hearts,

Little Alex MacDonald who was voted the outstanding player of the pre-season tournament at Ibrox

though they did trail by one goal at half time. Donald Park sneaked a goal five minutes before half time after Rangers had made almost all of the play until then.

Still, in the second half it was different. Two corner kicks from Tommy McLean caused a dramatic change in nine second half minutes. His first corner in fifty minutes found Alex MacDonald at the near post and his header flew into the net. Nine minutes later another corner from the little winger was finished off by Gordon Smith who scored with a header. It was all over then but just in case anyone had doubts Gordon Smith added a third a minute from the end. Rangers had run out easy winners and now faced the prospect of meeting Southampton, the team who had beaten them in the first of these annual tournaments two years earlier.

Southampton had looked very competent against West

31

It's Alex MacDonald in action again — this time against Celtic. Johannes Edvaldsson lunges in to tackle while Jim Casey stands by

Brom. They had an ordered look about their defence, the kind of look which suggested that they would not be giving goals away easily. And Rangers had failed against that kind of discipline before. The attackers from West Brom . . . Laurie Cunningham, Cyrille Regis, Willie Johnston and the rest had all been tied down securely by the Southampton tactics. Now Rangers would have to find a way through . . . .

But the worries the 32,000 Ibrox fans had over that disappeared in just twenty minutes of the final kicking off. Rangers' midfield took command and Alex MacDonald and Bobby Russell, destined to be key men right through the season, were the men who began to carve great gaps in the experienced Saints defence. Indeed it was one of these two architects who scored the opening goal in the twentieth minute . . . just as

The slim midfield ace Bobby Russell who scored a magnificent goal against Southampton as Rangers won their own tournament for the first time

good a goal as Ibrox saw during the whole of the season. Gordon Smith played a clever one-two with MacDonald before setting Russell free.

The slim, elegant, so-talented youngster carried the ball forward from just inside the Southampton half, looked up and then crashed a thirty yard shot into the net. It was a glorious start to a spell of attacking football which bewildered Southampton.

Eight minutes after that Smith set up another goal when he robbed a defender, pushed a ball inside and watched as Derek Parlane shot past the Southampton goalkeeper. Eight minutes more and Alex Forsyth, on loan from Old Trafford, scored his first goal for Rangers with a thundering drive from outside the box. Veteran striker Ted McDougall did get one back just before half time but Rangers were not in the mood to be denied. They were in command of the game and they stayed there with little Alex MacDonald scoring a fourth goal ten minutes from the end. That one reached the net just as press men in the box were voting MacDonald the man of the tournament!

He deserved that tag and the £100 which went with it. Even more, though, Rangers deserved to win the trophy at the third time of asking. John Greig had laid one of his personal jinxes and as well as that he had seen his team play the kind of football which he had demanded from them in all the pre-season training programmes. He admitted afterwards: 'It was time we won this tournament . . . but we wanted to play well too!'

They did both. And that Cup was the first of three they were to win during the longest season they had known . . . .

TAKING OVER FROM THE BOSS
by Ally Dawson

It isn't the easiest thing in the world to take over from a legend — and that's just about what I had to do when I broke into the Rangers first team last season!

Because it was my job as a left back to take over the jersey which our Boss John Greig had worn for so long as the club's captain. Yet, ironically, the injury which had almost cost me my chance of getting into the League side was probably the biggest help I had in overcoming my worries over taking the Boss's position.

When the directors appointed him as new Boss I felt that I would have the opportunity to get into the first team, a chance I had hoped for before but never been able to achieve. Then in pre-season training I was injured, suffered torn ligaments, and was left sitting in the stand watching Alex Forsyth, on loan from Manchester United, taking over the role I had dreamed about. At the time I felt terrible. I was sure that my chance had gone, that the injury had put me out of contention and that Alex would be able to slot in and make the place his own. I was right too. Alex did really well. He played in the European games against Juventus and PSV Eindhoven and as his confidence grew, mine withered a bit. Yet fitness came back and I returned to playing in the reserves — and that's where I began to feel less conscious of having to take over from the gaffer.

Eventually Alex was injured and I got my chance. But the fact that Alex had been in for that spell before me cushioned me from the worst of the worries. But it was still difficult not to be conscious of the fact that I was taking over from John Greig. People kept telling me that, they kept comparing the team with how it might have been if the manager was still playing. And I knew that it was impossible for me to step right in and take over where he left off. You're talking about a man who had been with Rangers for years, had skippered them for years, and had won trophy after trophy with the club down

Ally Dawson, the youngster who took over John Greig's left back position in the Rangers team

through those years. It was then that I decided I had to forget all about that and get on with my own job.

Having that extra spell in the reserves, having Alex Forsyth breaking the John Greig 'spell', all helped me to that decision. Probably it all paid off because soon I was being 'capped' for the Scotland Under-21 team, and I was in the Rangers team which won the League Cup and then the Scottish Cup.

It seemed fantastic to have that kind of success four whole years after making my debut in the first team! I suppose it's so long ago that some of the fans have forgotten that that is when I made my first appearance for Rangers. Of course, it was so far away from Ibrox that I wouldn't wonder that they had forgotten! You see I made my debut as a teenager in Vancouver on the first game of our round-the-world tour. We played the local team, Vancouver Whitecaps, and we won 4-0 despite it being our first ever taste of playing on the then new Astroturf. I was only in the team because a few of the regular players were on international duty with Scotland back home. Yet seven thousand miles away from Ibrox with only exiled fans to see me, I made my first appearance. It wasn't too long after I had been signed from the amateur team Easter-craigs. In fact I was still technically a schoolboy when I went on the trip which took us to Canada and then New Zealand and Australia. The manager at that time, Jock Wallace, spoke to me at Ibrox one night at training and asked me if I'd like to go on tour. Quite honestly I didn't realize that it was to be a twenty-seven day trek right around the world. When I did, it took quite a time for it all to sink in. Then I had to get permission from my school headmaster to leave early and so allow me to go with the team. It was a tremendous boost for me, a great lift to my early career with Rangers. To begin with, I was playing in the first team when I was still just a kid. And also, there is nothing like going on tour with a team to really get to know the lads. It makes it much easier for a youngster coming into the team if he has been abroad with the rest of the players beforehand. You spend a lot more time together than you would if you were at home and when I came back I wasn't a stranger any more.

But I wasn't a first team player either . . . .

There were one or two games for the top team, but mainly I was in the reserves serving the apprenticeship which everyone has to serve at Ibrox. I was in there learning my job as a professional footballer and the memories of that world tour faded as I got on with the job. It was good for me, too, because I was playing in a fairly experienced reserve squad, alongside men who could guide me a bit as I worked at my game.

Basically I didn't model myself on anyone at all. It was rather difficult for me because until I came to Ibrox I had always been played as a centre half. Then I was drafted into the left back position, although I'm more right footed than anything else. So who could I watch?

In the end I suppose what I have done is try to take a little bit from all the players I admire. When I am playing now, being mainly right sided I tend to look more closely at those who are in the same position but are left footed.

Leeds United's Frankie Gray who has been in the Scotland team has impressed me. He is naturally left sided, of course,

Hibs' experienced sweeper Jacky McNamara slides in to tackle Rangers'
left back Ally Dawson as the youngster bursts forward into attack

and so I like to see what he does when he is going forward and
what positions he tends to drop into while defending. On the
other side of the field I don't think there is any better player in
Scotland than Sandy Jardine my Ibrox team-mate. When he is
going forward he is superb and he is a good defender too,
which people are inclined to forget. The thing about Sandy is
he reads the game so well that he can play himself out of tight
situations magnificently.

I like going forward myself but because of my days as a
centre half I like to think that I can tackle a bit too. But there
are parts of my game which are not as strong as I'd like them to
be and I try to work on them fairly hard. My heading for
example could be better so I practise that. Then I also practise
getting to the bye-line and crossing the ball. It is a move which
can cause danger to any defence but I feel my crosses are too
weak and I'll be brushing up on this part of my game until I
feel fairly confident about that left foot of mine.

It's all very well talking about going forward, but you have to
be able to defend. Also you have to be able to cope with all
kinds of different wingers nowadays. I suppose every full back
has a problem opponent and I'm no different . . . maybe I have

A determined-looking Ally Dawson moves clear with the ball as St
Mirren's Frank McGarvey, now with Liverpool, comes in to challenge

one or two! Yet in my own mind there is one player who gives me more problems than anyone else and that's Bobby Houston of Partick Thistle. He isn't an orthodox winger, not an out and out winger in the old-fashioned sense of the word. Unfortunately he does play wide and he is my responsibility whenever we have to play Thistle. I suppose because his team tends to play a defensive formation, Houston lies very deep. If you go back there with him then he lobs it over the top of you into the space you have left and their front men can move in. Even when they are playing down the other flank he still lies off you, still lurks around deep. If you don't go to him then he can pick the ball up and cause damage that way. It's a problem I'm still working on after coming up against him several times last season!

While he gives me regular problems, the best I've come up against is probably Roger van Gool, the Belgian international outside right who played for Cologne of West Germany in the European Cup quarter finals against us at Ibrox. He is a great player and he took us a bit by surprise because we didn't know too much about him. He had come back from injury to play against us and he was very, very hard to pin down. Great pace and tremendous control, and he gave Nottingham Forest a lot of problems when they played Cologne in that epic semi-final at the City Ground in Nottingham.

I suppose that was one of my major disappointments last season — going out of the European Cup to Cologne, I mean — because the team had done so well in the opening two rounds that we were beginning to believe that we could win the trophy and, naturally, that's the ambition of every man at Ibrox. The other disappointment was losing the Premier League title. Although I won two medals last season I want to get a championship medal this year. All the lads were upset about losing that crucial game to Celtic and even winning the Scottish Cup a week later didn't ease the disappointment any. Still, we just have to get on with things and make sure we don't let down the fans again this coming year.

The League Cup Final against Aberdeen brought me my first medal. That will always remain memorable to me. It was my first Cup Final, probably the biggest crowd I'd ever played in front of and thanks to Colin Jackson's header we won and I got my first ever medal.

Then came the Scottish Cup and that long running battle with Hibs. Three games altogether, plus sessions of extra time in two of them before we eventually won that one. So to get my two medals I actually played in *four* Cup Finals. That's

An action shot of Dawson as he starts off on attacking run

probably something for the *Guiness Book of Records*, and certainly one of those questions that usually turn up in quiz games. You know the kind — 'Who played in four Cup Finals in his first season in Rangers' first team and won two medals?'

The last of the three Scottish Cup games against Hibs was the best. It had so much excitement and I enjoyed it too because the Boss switched me in the first half to take over a marking role and I always feel quite happy doing that kind of job. We were a goal down when he decided to change the team, pushing Derek Johnstone up front, taking Sandy Jardine into a sweeper position which he plays so well, and using me on the right against Tony Higgins. He is another man who is awkward to play against because he is so big and strong. But I enjoyed battling it out with him . . . .

And, in the end, it was another medal. One which means that we will be in the European Cup Winners' Cup next season. I hope that we get a fairly long run because the Boss always underlines how important it is for the club to be admired in Europe and that's what we have to aim for. Personally, too, I welcome the chance to get a crack at some of the foreign clubs again. I went abroad a few times with the youth team at Ibrox and I found it fascinating to come up against the various styles of play that the other countries use. Now I have learned a little at senior level with Rangers and with the Scotland Under-21 team, I just want to go on learning. I think that playing in Europe at any level helps make you a better player. Your technique improves, you begin to see that there is so much more to football than the little bit you happen to play in, and all in all you should become a better player. I hope I do because that way I could achieve the two or three ambitions I have left . . . winning a full Scotland cap and helping win the Premier League and the European Cup!

OUT GO THE DUTCH

Forty-eight hours after the second round draw for the European Cup had pushed Rangers into a clash with PSV Eindhoven of Holland I was with John Greig in the Feyenoord Stadium in Rotterdam.

It was there on that bitterly cold Sunday afternoon that Greig compiled his Eindhoven dossier. He did so as he watched PSV go down 1-0 to Feyenoord in a Dutch First Division match. Thirty-eight thousand people watched that game — and all of them realized that PSV had had an off day. It didn't deceive any of the Dutch fans and it didn't deceive Greig either. The Dutch team boss Jan Zwartkruis — he had succeeded Ernst Happel after the World Cup Final — told Greig: 'This was not the real form of PSV. They can play so very much better than they did against Feyenoord. That is why so many of their team were with us in Argentina . . . .'

In fact, six of the PSV players were in the Dutch World Cup squad — another, Willy van der Kuylen, turned down the opportunity to play in Argentina — and four of them played in the Final in Buenos Aires.

These four were the twins Willy and Rene van der Kerkhof, Ernie Brandts and Jan Portvliet while the other two were Harry Lubse and Arie van Kraaj. Greig knew of their Argentina displays and after the Feyenoord match he told me simply: 'They had a bit of an off day against Feyenoord — but that doesn't make them a bad team. In some ways it will be even more difficult playing against them than it was playing against Juventus.

'They are not a team like the Italians. It was fairly easy, for example, to play man-for-man marking against Juventus because their players are disciplined to remain in their own areas. That kind of tactic would be impossible against a Dutch team. They have the fluidity you have learned to expect from Dutch football. Call it total football, if you like. It is the same kind of game that Ajax used against us a few years back — and the same the Dutch national team uses.

43

An earlier meeting between one of Rangers' World Cup players, Tom
Forsyth, and one of PSV Eindhoven's Argentina stars, Willy van der
Kerkhof. Here the Dutchman tackles Forsyth in the World Cup clash
which Scotland won 3 — 2 in Mendoza

'Their players switch about, they don't remain in specific
areas and I wouldn't think of going into the games against
them using man-for-man marking. It would end up with my
players being pulled into bad positions. So, it calls for a fresh
approach, completely different from the Juventus tie.

'I did see one or two things I may be able to capitalize on.
Their defence is not outstanding in the air and they were
caught square at the back once or twice. That's something for
us to work on . . . .'

As well as these encouraging signs there were more hopeful
hints for Rangers as the first leg at Ibrox — yet another 44,000
sell-out — approached. Rene van der Kerkhof was doubtful
through injury and his brother Willy was hurt playing in an
international for Holland the week before the Dutch were

Harry Lubse, one of the six Dutch World Cup men in the PSV side in action in a First Division match in Holland. He scored in thirty-four seconds of the dramatic second leg European Cup game between Rangers and the Dutch champions

scheduled to arrive in Glasgow. It was a problem for the small Dutch coach Cees Rijvers, but it was scarcely an insurmountable one, for the team from Eindhoven's aim at Ibrox was to survive without losing a goal.

Rijvers admitted as much when the team flew into Glasgow. Smilingly he admitted: 'It must be a defensive approach, just as it was for Rangers when they went to Turin in the last round. Europe is made this way, although we shall be trying to score one goal. Away goals are important in the tournament and we are aware of this.'

On the night five of the World Cup men played — only Rene van der Kerkhof was missing. Rijvers had devised a deep defensive strategy, using the offside trap the Dutch rely on so much in all their football, and then looking to hit Rangers on

Derek Parlane is the lone Ranger in this picture from the first leg game against PSV in Glasgow. There are four Dutch defenders with him but the Ibrox striker gets in his shot. Unfortunately he couldn't score and the game ended 0-0

the break. Yet the offside trap almost rebounded on them in the opening minutes of the game. At Largs Greig had warned his players of this tactic and urged them to hold the ball and go it alone if they saw the Dutch charge forward. Tom Forsyth did just that, reached the penalty box and then as the goalkeeper came off his line sent the kick wide. It was a miss Rangers were to regret . . . .

Indeed it was the best chance they had in the game and inspired them to a superbly confident and creative opening burst which had the usually cool Dutchmen showing signs of panic.

Alex MacDonald might have scored, so too might Bobby Russell and the vastly experienced Willy van der Kerkhof almost conceded an own goal with a despairing attempt to clear as Rangers powered forward. It was what the fans wanted to see and when firstly van der Kuylen and then van der Kerkhof, in the second half, both had to be substituted, the Scottish champions seemed on target for a convincing win.

Gradually, however, the momentum of these Rangers raids slackened. Ernie Brandts began to master Derek Johnstone in

46

Rangers' striker Derek Johnstone in an aerial duel with PSV defender Arie van Kraaj . . . one of their World Cup men

the air, the Dutch grew more confident as the game wore on. And when goalkeeper van Engelen made a magnificent save from Bobby Russell late in the second half it was obvious that this was not going to be a night when Rangers and their fans would celebrate a famous victory. The game dragged to an end without a goal being scored and left Rangers facing an even more difficult job than they had in the second leg game against Juventus a few weeks earlier.

Then they had to score goals at home — now they had to score goals away from home. And they had to do it against a team who had never lost at home in a single European tie over a tournament span of more than twenty years!

There was no doubting Greig's disappointment although defiantly he told me: 'It just means that we have to get a result in Holland. We made enough chances to win but were that bit unlucky. Now we have to take chances in the next leg and, remember, any scoring draw will carry us into the quarter finals.'

While Greig remained stubbornly optimistic the Dutch were jubilant. They had believed it possible from the beginning that they could win the European Cup and follow up their triumph in the UEFA Cup at the end of the previous season. Now with a draw in Glasgow they saw little to stop them crashing into the tournament's last eight.

Their star players, Willy and Rene van der Kerkhof were both ready for the return and both told me on the eve of the game just how confident they felt.

Said Willy: 'We are the best-equipped team left in the European Cup. I think we can win this competition. Rangers are a good team but they are still a little bit short of being a top class European side. Remember, too, that we have never lost a European match at home. We don't intend to start doing so now . . . .'

And Rene added: 'I did not play in the Glasgow game but I was there to watch it. Last season I saw Rangers against FC Twente in Enschede when they went out. Now they are a better team. To be honest I underestimated them before we went to Glasgow. Some of their midfield play was tremendous. MacDonald and McLean and Russell played very well.

'They varied the play a lot in the first half but towards the end I thought they dropped back into bad habits. They did what so many British teams do, just hit high balls into goal.

'I doubt if they have the discipline of the best Continental teams. They won't show the same patience as we would be prepared to do.'

48

A duel between two of Scotland's
brightest midfield men and
Rangers' Robert Russell comes out
on top against Celtic's Tommy Burns

Right: Bobby Russell rises above Celtic captain Danny McGrain in this Old Firm clash

Opposite left: Alex MacDonald stretches for the ball in the Cup Final against Hibs

Opposite right: Davie Cooper torments Ally Brazil just as he did in all three of the Cup Final clashes against Hibs

Opposite below: It's the first game of the three and Robert Russell swerves away from the Hibs defence

Below: Rangers have scored in the Hampden league match and the players turn away to celebrate

Left: Young Ally Dawson, on the way to his first medal, beats Aberdeen's strong man defender Doug Rougvie to this ball in the League Cup Final at Hampden

Opposite above: Alex MacDonald turns away, arms upraised, after he has scored Rangers' opening goal against Juventus at Ibrox. Italian defender Marco Tardelli tries to clear — but he's too late!

Opposite below: Rangers' striker Derek Parlane carries the ball past Celtic's Johannes Edvaldsson in one of the Old Firm matches last season

Below left: John McMaster challenges Gordon Smith in the League Cup Final

Below right: Ally Dawson, the man who made John Greig's old left back position his own

Opposite left: An action shot of Rangers' skipper Derek Johnstone

Opposite right: Sandy Jardine, one of the most consistent players at Ibrox last season

Opposite below: A clash between two wingers as Davie Cooper of Rangers and Davie Provan of Celtic face up to each other

Above left: Little Tommy McLean whose skill helped Rangers so much in Europe last season

Above right: Ibrox giant goalkeeper Peter McCloy lines up for one of his famous long clearances

Right: Alex MacDonald and Kenny Watson combine to squeeze out Celtic's Murdo MacLeod

In the end both agreed that PSV would win the game and Rene believed that they would do so by two goals. It was a belief shared by most of Europe. But, then, surely this was Rangers' season to confound an entire continent!

But they had to go into the game with a change from their so successful European line-up of the first round. Colin Jackson, hurt at Ibrox against the Dutchmen, was still out despite a fitness test on the day of the match. Derek Johnstone went to centre half and the team was: McCloy; Jardine, A Forsyth; T. Forsyth, Johnstone, MacDonald; McLean, Russell, Parlane, Smith, Watson.

The Dutch lined up without van der Kuylen but with all six of their Argentinian stars. Their team was: van Engelen; Krijgh, Stevens, van Kraaj, Brandts, W. van der Kerkhof, Jansen, Portvliet, R. van der Kerkhof, Lubse, Deijkers.

Twenty-nine thousand people were in the tight PSV Stadium as the teams kicked off and within 34 seconds they had seen the Dutch cracks go in front. That was all the time which had ticked away on the giant stadium clock when Harry Lubse crashed a spectacular shot past Peter McCloy to silence the Rangers fans in the crowd. It was the same kind of start as Rangers had had in Turin — only the loss of an early goal arrived earlier this time — and it was what Greig had wanted to avoid. Somehow, though, it was now that Rangers drew on all their reserves of courage and skill, now that they decided they would not buckle down, they would not crumble after what might have been a killer blow. With Alex MacDonald inspiring them they gathered themselves, picked themselves up and began to play the controlled football Greig had demanded from them.

They pushed forward, showing the kind of patience the van der Kerkhofs were convinced would desert them. They stuck to the system laid down by team boss Greig even when they failed to get an equaliser before half time. Twice they came close and twice Tony van Engelen saved from Derek Parlane and Alex Forsyth.

But the goal they deserved did come. Twelve minutes after half time Alex MacDonald, thrusting at the heart of the Dutch defence like some red-tipped dagger, headed the Scots level from a Tommy McLean cross. Yet within three minutes the Ibrox team were behind again when a glorious attacking move left their defence in tatters allowing Gerry Deijkers to score with a shot from a dozen yards out.

Now the real test came as these Rangers players had to fight back for a second time. Derek Parlane missed one magnificent

Rangers' midfield man Bobby
Russell

It's Derek Johnstone again, challenging powerfully for the ball along with Ernie Brandts who starred for Holland against Argentina in the World Cup Final

Alex MacDonald in mid-air as he hits a shot for goal against PSV Eindhoven at Ibrox

chance and then in 66 minutes they were back in a match-winning position. McLean was the goal-maker again, slipping a free kick to Kenny Watson on the edge of the penalty box. He hammered the ball for goal and, at the last second, Derek Johnstone reached it and with a flick of his head turned it out of the keeper's reach and into the corner of the goal.

PSV hit the panic button now. Ernie Brandts was pushed upfield and the high balls they had criticized Rangers for using were being rained in on the Scots penalty box. Somehow Rangers survived this barrage and three minutes from the end a move of rare precision ended the contest. It was little Tommy McLean once more, picking the ball up on the right and then curling it past a defender into the path of young Bobby Russell. He strode clear of the Dutch defence, drew the keeper from his line and then placed it perfectly past him and into the net. It was the winner and Rangers' fans roared their songs of joy from the terracings. Songs which continued long after the final whistle and which echoed around the darkened stadium as they waited outside to cheer their heroes.

And these eleven players were heroes. Every one of them. Manager Greig laid it on the line when he said: 'I have never known a better performance in Europe than this one as long as I have been with the club. The players were out of this world.

'I always felt we had a chance in the tie. But then we lost that early goal. And, after we equalised, we lost another very quickly. But the team persisted in playing football. They kept playing the game the way we had planned it and they got the pay off they deserved. I couldn't be more delighted for the players.'

And Greig was not alone in praising his men. Former Ajax and Dutch international team boss Rinus Michels, who was also manager of Barcelona, watched the game. Afterwards he told me: 'Rangers surprised me a little because the game they played was more European-styled than we have come to expect from British teams. When any team is able to beat first Juventus and then PSV Eindhoven, then they have to be looked on as major contenders for the trophy.'

That was a conclusion that the Rangers fans were ready to draw from the results, too. Yet it wasn't something that Greig welcomed. He looked at the other teams in the last eight, began to study their results and remembered previous disappointments. 'You can't talk about winning a tournament after just two rounds,' he warned. 'But it is a good thing to get past the second round again. That's the first time we have managed it since we won the European Cup Winners' Cup in 1972.

Little Tommy McLean, architect of the victory over PSV in Eindhoven, sends over one of those perfect crosses — exactly the kind of ball which caught out the Dutch!

When we did that we played top teams all the way through and that's happened so far in this one. I wouldn't mind it continuing in the quarter finals. I do believe that we are at our best when we are playing against a fancied team.'

It was hard not to recall that march through Europe of seven seasons earlier when Rangers beat Rennes of France, Sporting Club of Portugal, FC Torino of Italy, Bayern Munich of West Germany and then Moscow Dynamo in that Barcelona final of the Cup Winners' Cup. As the fans and players were held up in fog bound Amsterdam the day after the game, Schipol Airport buzzed with memories of that season. Then the names of the remaining quarter finalists were thrown up — Nottingham Forest of England, Cologne of West Germany,

Malmo of Sweden, Grasshoppers Zurich of Switzerland, Wisla Cracow of Poland, Dynamo Dresden of East Germany and FK Austria, the Viennese champions of Austria.

Rangers were able to boast more European experience than any of them. Peter McCloy, Sandy Jardine, Derek Johnstone, Alex MacDonald and Tommy McLean had all played in Barcelona while Colin Jackson and Derek Parlane had been in the Europe squad then.

Yet talk of the European Cup had to be postponed as the tournament went on ice for a couple of months before the draw was made in Zurich; then, for a further two months before the quarter final ties, scheduled for March.

That gave Greig and his players time to concentrate on the domestic front as they bid to hold onto the treble they had won the year before. All the time, though, the challenge of Europe with its excitement, with its very special sense of occasion, hung tantalisingly in front of them. Two famous scalps had been taken and the players fretted to be back among the big names and display again just how Rangers had grown up in Europe.

THERE'S NOT A TEAM...
by Andy Cameron

Who's that team they call the Rangers? For me they're the only team in football . . .

Never mind the Bluenose bit, I've been a Rangers fan for thirty-five years and I still can't see past them.

Don't worry about it, I had to battle to graduate as a Teddy Bear for my grandfather introduced me to football, and he was a Clyde supporter. Obviously he wasn't too well educated. Not only that, he wouldn't allow parties in the house because the big crowds frightened him!

My very first memory of the Rangers dates back to 1945 when we drew 2-2 with Moscow Dynamo. I was only five at the time, but I recall my uncle lifting me over the turnstile and saying: 'You'll need to keep your eye on this bloke John Greig . . . .'

Only joking, John came along a couple of years after that. I double-checked with Arthur Negus.

Over the years I've gone from being 'lifted over' at Ibrox to a season ticket-holder, but I'd hate to think I've any less enthusiasm when it comes to shouting on the side. No way. Like every other punter I think I talk a good game — in between arguments!

For instance, my all-time favourite Rangers side revolves around the 60s when Eric Caldow and company did a fair bit of damage. The team was (altogether now) — Ritchie, Shearer, Caldow, Greig, McKinnon, Baxter, Henderson, McMillan, Millar, Brand and Wilson.

How that team didn't win the European Cup I'll never know . . . in that side you had a better mixture than Bassett's liquorice allsorts.

For starters the full backs were like chalk and cheese — Captain Cutlass at No.2 and the slightly more cultured Caldow at No.3. There was the blend of Greig, McKinnon and Baxter at half back. Different class. And up front the speed of Henderson, the skill of McMillan, the heart of Millar, the scoring touch of Brand and the direct play of Wilson.

54

Contrary to rumours Davy Wilson didn't 'dive' as often as Jacques Cousteau, but if you happened to trip him in the centre circle the chances were he fell in the penalty area!

As it happens my favourite Rangers player is one of the 60s side. And before you jump the gun, it's not Jim Baxter. For me Jimmy Millar typifies what a Rangers player is all about. He had guts, determination and more ability than he was given credit for. Plus the fact he could play in any position. Like John Greig he was one of the few players Celtic fans respected . . . or loved to hate.

Another thing I admired about Millar was his attitude. He didn't fall about when he was tackled or chirp at the referee when he was fouled. Jimmy got on with it. His motto on occasions was 'Cut out the football and get on with the game . . . .'

Recently I met Jimmy Millar at a function, and I couldn't get over the fact that I still felt like a wee boy when I was talking to him. Okay, I admit it, I asked him for his autograph. He said: 'Nae bother Sydney, and by the way my wife loves your ell-pees!'

Of course when you talk about skill, you've got to talk about guys like Baxter and McMillan and nowadays Robert Russell and Tommy McLean. All four can do everything but make the ball talk, and that's got to be down to natural ability.

The game has changed since the Baxter-McMillan era, but it's encouraging to see that Rangers still rely on skilful players. Wee McLean is an architect in the true football sense. Actually, I've known him since he was a hod-carrier with Lego.

The first time I saw him play he was centre half in a Sub-buteo Select. Since then he's graduated to being a hit-man for the Brownies in Larkhall, not to mention his job as a chucker-out in Mothercare.

Seriously, he and Robert Russell have great 'vision' — that's the current jargon. They make other people play, and that's what a team game is all about. Russell has impressed me with his ability and his honesty. He paid me back two quid he owed me just last week!

The 'honesty' I'm on about is the fact that he doesn't hide in games even when he isn't playing well. He's always looking for the ball. For me young Robert has been one of the best football finds in ages.

When I get talking with my pals about Rangers best-ever performance since the war the majority come down on the side of '72 when we lifted the European Cup Winners' Cup in Barcleona, beating Moscow Dynamo 3-2. I don't go along with that . . . .

Andy Cameron

Again I'll harp back to the Ritchie, Shearer, Caldow team because the best-ever team performance I saw came from ten men in Light Blue jerseys at Tynecastle!

I recall Ritchie was carried off early doors . . . Shearer went in goal . . . Rangers went a goal behind . . . and ended up winning the match 3-1. Now that takes a bit of beating.

Obviously winning the European Cup Winners' Cup was the club's greatest triumph. However, the distinction has had to take second place to the 'riot' which followed the match. Personally, I think the Spanish police over-reacted — and so too did the media! If the game had been played anywhere other than Spain I don't think there would have been anything like the trouble.

I managed to get to that game with a little bit of luck because I won a competition in the *Scottish Daily Express*. It was a tremendous performance by Rangers that night, and I was particularly pleased for John Greig.

Greig carried the team for years and by rights he should be a hunchback today. Which reminds me of the round-shouldered guy who took a shy in a game and threw himself into the middle of the park . . . .

The fact that John Greig has made the transition from player to manager as easily as he has done is a tribute in itself to the man. Basically, he knows the game and believe it or not, that helps.

But let's face it, he could never have been a filmstar with a face like that. Well, maybe with Hammer Films because his hobby is haunting houses. Fortunately, I know John well and he has a sense of humour. If you passed a ball the way he did you needed a sense of humour.

I think it's obvious Greig is gearing Rangers towards another European victory. The wins over Juventus and Eindhoven last season prove that. In fact, I rate the 3-2 win over the Dutch side in Holland as the best football I've seen from Rangers in all the time I've been spectating.

Not that my football knowledge is confined to watching. I did a fair bit of playing in the Churches League (playing, not praying) and filled in as a Tiger Shaw-type full back. Like John Greig I could cross a good winger . . . .

But the people who make football are undoubtedly the punters. And it wouldn't do the players of every team any harm to be reminded from time to time that they're the guys who pay the wages.

Rangers have a tremendous support. Never mind the head-bangers because no way are they fans — and just about every club has its share — I'm talking about men and women who follow — follow — follow.

Two of the most ardent Rangers fans I know are Jimmy Clark and Andy Bain. If either of them misses a game the *Guinness Book of Records* is informed. You name it and they've seen it if it involves Light Blue jerseys.

Jimmy Clark has been running buses from Bridgeton Cross for as long as I can remember. If Rangers were playing in Uganda this week and Glasgow Green the next there would still be a bus. Now that's a bit special.

Andy Bain is your actual Rangers regular. If he doesn't appear for a game you can bet the team won't turn up. I kid him on about being a war veteran because he lost a leg in the war. You don't need to ask — it was his left one!

It's with punters like Jimmy and Andy, not to mention you and me, in mind that I hope to see Rangers making their mark in Europe again, and when Derek Johnstone lifts the Cup I'd like to think not one fan is lifted with it.

Here's to a red-white-and-blue 1980!

THE EUROPE DREAM DIES

When the draw was made for the quarter finals of the European Cup in the plush surroundings of the Atlantis Hotel in Zurich, the entire Continent was agreed upon one thing — Rangers had earned themselves one of the easier draws!

Yet, somehow, the fates did not see it that way. After disposing of Juventus, after being too good for PSV Eindhoven, Rangers were paired with the champions of West Germany, Cologne.

It was another tough one, another game which meant an Ibrox sell out as soon as the tickets went on sale, another game which captured the imagination of the Rangers fans. But it was also one of the hardest hurdles left for any team remaining in the tournament of champions. Ibrox boss John Greig knew that, and, if he did have any doubts about the task, the problems were underlined for him by Europe's Footballer of the Year Kevin Keegan. The England star, now the hero of Hamburg, helped Greig build a dossier on his opponents. He told him, too: 'If Rangers can beat Cologne after having beaten Juventus and Eindhoven already, then they should just be handed the European Cup. Because, really, they will have done more than enough to win the trophy!'

That's how Keegan saw the job facing Rangers and when Greig went to see them twice before the first tie in West Germany he realized that this was to be even harder than the previous two epic ties. He saw them play first against lowly placed Bundesliga team Darmstadt and then again, just before the first game, against the West German league leaders Kaiserslautern. In the matches he did see flaws he hoped to exploit ... but also he saw a team coming back to greatness. The year before, under the expert guidance of Hennes Weisweiller their vastly experienced coach, Cologne had won the League and Cup double. Then at the beginning of the season they had failed to live up to the high hopes their fans had of them. As the tie approached they were in eighth place in the Bundesliga and they had had problems. The major worry had been over a

The man Rangers manager John Greig decided was the 'danger man' of Cologne, midfield general Heinz Flohe, seen here in action for West Germany's international team

Three views of the goal which meant Rangers' hopes of European Cup glory had ended — Cologne striker Dieter Muller beats centre half Colin Jackson to the ball and sends his header for goal

leg injury to Heinz Flohe their World Cup star who was rated the finest playmaker in West Germany.

And the secondary worry was the scoring failure of another World Cup man, striker Dieter Muller, who had managed to score just twice in the West German championship before the first meeting with Rangers.

Yet, by the time Greig saw them, Flohe had shaken off his injury worries. After a succession of different treatments from a succession of eminent specialists, his muscle injury had been cured. Keegan had warned that Cologne were a different team when Flohe was in — and especially when he was on song. Greig soon saw that for himself. After the game in Darmstadt he admitted to me: 'It's all about Flohe with them. He is the man who makes them tick. Everything is channelled through him and he is a very, very influential player in their line up.

'I can understand why they would not be so potent without him because it is almost as if they rely on him on the field. Yet

Muller is still with Jackson at the right hand post as goalkeeper Peter McCloy scrambles along his line — but the ball has beaten him

It's all over, Peter McCloy is on the ground while defender Tom Forsyth looks on glumly and West German star Bernd Cullmann turns away with his arms raised in triumph

they have other good players ... Herbert Zimmermann is superb, and Herbert Neumann and Harald Kanopka. I knew they would be good, of course. I've played many times against West German teams, both with Rangers and Scotland, and I've always had a great respect for them.

'In many ways they combine the best qualities of the Italians and the Dutch. They have the discipline of the Italians and the flair that Holland has brought back into the game. So it will be like playing Juventus and PSV rolled into one.

'Yet they do look vulnerable to cross balls at the back. Someone like Derek Johnstone will be able to take advantage of this . . . .'

Johnstone, of course, had been marked down by Cologne as the danger to their hopes. Weisweiller had told me: 'Johnstone is a danger to our team, both my coaches who have seen Rangers believe this and I do too from what I have seen on film. He must be curbed if we are to do anything against Rangers ....'

That is why the worst European blow Rangers received was an injury to Johnstone just a few weeks before the first leg — an injury serious enough to keep the captain out of that vital opening tie in the Mungersdorf Stadium!

It was a cruel blow to Greig and his planning and a boost for Weisweiller who had looked on the tie with fear. A genuine fear at that. The man who had bossed Borussia Moenchengladbach in their glory days in Europe, and then Barcelona where he had a much publicised feud with Johan Cruyff, had a respect for British football. Rangers' results had strengthened that respect and he admitted to me before the first leg: 'I like the directness of British football and I admire the players' fitness and their determination. Your teams — and I know this is especially true of Rangers — will never give up in a game. When everything seems lost they still fight on and this is something we find hard to instil into our own German teams.

'I did not want to play Rangers in the tournament and I did not want to play Nottingham Forest either. I would have preferred them to play each other and eliminate one of the dangers to us. But we have Heinz Flohe back and if Dieter Muller can begin to score goals again things will be right for us.

'The lack of goals concerns me, it concerns Dieter, and it concerns everyone in Cologne. You have seen him and he is suffering the way only strikers can suffer. Some of this is due to the World Cup, I think. Dieter has lost confidence and he must get it back.

'A lot has been said to me about the way Rangers played

The consolation for Rangers. The Cologne line-up is still disorganized as Tommy McLean (number 7) floats in the free kick equaliser at Ibrox. Other Rangers players in the picture are Sandy Jardine (2) and Davie Cooper (11).

against Juventus and PSV Eindhoven. I admire these results. I am impressed by them. But they are in the past now. These results are behind Rangers and this game will be decided on which of our two teams is best on the night. I'm sure John Greig agrees with that.'

Greig did. Part of his job was to play down the previous successes and emphasize the qualities of Cologne. Just as Juventus and PSV had had their share of World Cup heroes, so had the West Germans. They had five men who had gone to Argentina with Helmut Schoen — defenders Harald Kanopka and Herbert Zimmermann, midfield men Bernd Cullmann and Heinz Flohe and striker Dieter Muller. A formidable five!

Yet none of them were safe from Weisweiller's demands. The coach, known as the scourge of the stars, did not allow anyone to live on their reputations. Gunter Netzer had learned that at Moenchengladbach when Weisweiller sold him; Cruyff had learned it in a bitter feud at Barcelona, and Wolfgang Overath had been dropped the previous season and had retired because he could not work under the ruthless veteran.

Now the man who had Weisweiller's wrath turned on him

63

was Muller. By Weisweiller's standards he had been patient with his non-scoring striker — but on the eve of the first game against Rangers, Muller came under threat.

I was in Cologne to see them play Kaiserslautern. They went two goals ahead and then lost the lead late in the game and finished up drawing 2-2. The defence looked bad and Muller was able to score — his second of the season in League games — but it wasn't enough to satisfy Weisweiller. Afterwards he stormed: 'Muller has not done enough for us this season. One goal against Kaiserslautern does not make up for the misses he has had this season.

'If he does not score against Rangers then there will be no place for him with the club. It is as simple as that. He has not convinced me that his form is back and he must do that or he will leave. I have given him enough time.'

It was a clear ultimatum served on the star who was Cologne's highest-paid player, a man who drove to training in a Mercedes, who lived in a luxury home, and who picked up a salary of around £80,000 a year. And it was done in a bid to make sure that Muller would give his best in the game which suddenly mattered most of all to Weisweiller and his team — the European Cup clash with Rangers!

Besides the scoring problems of Muller the team had lost bad goals against the League leaders. Greig had seen them and had been heartened. Weisweiller was furious. He told me: 'If they are as bad in defence against Rangers, if they are as careless and as slack, then we can forget the European Cup!'

Yet Weisweiller's worries were nothing compared to those facing Rangers. As well as Derek Johnstone's enforced absence as he went through a leg operation, Rangers arrived in the cathedral city on the Rhine with more injury problems. Midfield man Kenny Watson was out; Tom Forsyth, Alex MacDonald, Tommy McLean and Derek Parlane were doubt-ful for one reason or another and the Scottish champions prepared for the game with their hopes of reaching the Munich final already beginning to fade.

And twenty-four hours before the match, with the doubts remaining, Greig became involved in a bitter pre-match row with the West German club's officials.

When Rangers arrived for training at the Mungersdorf Stadium an official refused to allow them onto the playing pitch. Only after Greig and his vice-chairman Willie Waddell demanded to see the Cologne general manager Karl Heinz Thielen and read him the European Cup competition rules, were Rangers allowed to train. It states clearly in the rules that

Gordon Smith is beaten to this ball by the quick tackling Cologne full back Harald Kanopka, as the Ibrox man tries to burst into attack

Alex MacDonald is the Scot trying to get clear here as he is tackled by Cologne players Bernd Cullmann on the ground and Herbert Neumann

Rangers' captain for the night, Sandy Jardine, congratulates Cologne star Herbert Zimmermann at the end of the Ibrox game.

a team must be allowed to train on the match pitch twenty-four hours before the tie. Greig, trying to combat his injury problems, was furious. He stormed: 'It was ridiculous. They tried to say there had been overnight rain which made the surface of the pitch difficult. But the ground was perfect when the players worked out. I was very disappointed with the attitude of the Germans.

'They were trying to mess us about. I'm sure of that and the players feel the same. I think it has increased their determination to get a result. But we still have injuries worrying us.'

In the end Greig did field as close to the full team as he could ... risking little Tommy McLean, though he was still suffering badly from gastro-enteritis, and pushing Tom Forsyth and Alex MacDonald through demanding fitness tests before getting the all clear from them. Twenty-four hours before the match he summed it up this way: 'Cologne are not as good a team as Juventus, but then I don't think we will meet another team as good as the Italian champions even if we reach the Final. But I have one hundred per cent respect for West German football. I respect them more than any other country possibly because I have played so often against their teams myself. We have to be patient here — and disciplined. We have to look for a good result, naturally, and a scoring draw would be fine for us.'

There was just one surprise in Greig's team selection, with Jim Denny coming into the defence, allowing Sandy Jardine to shadow Flohe wherever the West German star decided to go. And how well Jardine played! He was one of Rangers' giants on a night when all their heroes were in defence. Forty-five thousand fans were in the Cologne stadium for the game and they saw a backs-to-the-wall Rangers, a display of guts and determination and sheer defiance from a team which had faced too many worries to be at their best. There was no repeat of Eindhoven. Instead it was a little like that opening match in Turin, though Rangers had to fight even harder for survival.

They survived just enough to keep their chances alive for the second leg at Ibrox, going down by 1-0. The goal was scored by Dieter Muller, the star who had been threatened with the axe by Weisweiller if he could not score against the Scots. The threat worked in the fifty-seventh minute as Rangers' defence, for once in the game, collapsed under the relentless pressure. A ball which should have been cleared, and which could have been cleared, bobbed about in the penalty box before Muller reached it to head a ball just inside

Peter McCloy's right hand post. The tall goalkeeper had been one of Rangers' best players, stringing together save after save and in the closing minutes he stopped a Flohe effort magnificently. In front of him Tom Forsyth was another star, relishing the pressure that the West Germans placed him and his mates under for so many of the ninety minutes. Then, too, there was Sandy Jardine, curbing Flohe, taking on the hardest job on the field and peforming superbly against the Cologne playmaker.

That one goal was all Cologne could manage and Greig knew that his chances of getting through to the semi-finals had improved. He admitted as much on the flight home when he told me: 'I was worried before the game because of all the injury problems but things went a little bit our way. We might have been beaten by more and now the initiative has come to us. They wanted more than just one goal. But, at the same time, they are in front. Our fans have to realize that. It's a good result, but we did lose the game and we have a job on our hands at Ibrox!'

The injuries persisted for the second leg ... Johnstone was in training but not one hundred per cent while Watson was still out as was reserve centre Chris Robertson. And Derek Parlane was hurt too. Young Billy Urquhart, signed from the Highland League at the start of the season, was the sole striker left who was fully fit.

Cologne had team changes in mind and one of them was to bring in the Belgian international winger Roger van Gool who had been missing from the first match. But Weisweiller wanted a change in the normal attitude too. He insisted: 'We cannot sit on a one goal lead. That will be too dangerous for us. We must try to get something out of the game. If we can score then we will win the tie!'

Greig listened to the comments from his vastly experienced opposite number and decided to shroud his own team in secrecy. Said Greig: 'Weisweiller is a fox, a very cunning old fox, and he will have something up his sleeve for us. I know that now. I have to try to be as big a fox as him. Any advantage I can get I'll take because I know that Cologne will pose us problems, more problems than Juventus did when they came here in exactly the same situation. The Italians might have better players but they were stereotyped, predictable, and I don't think Cologne will be that. He will bring his team to Ibrox looking for a goal.'

The German captain Heinz Flohe had decided that he wanted revenge for a score he had to settle from twelve years earlier. 'I played here for Cologne in the old Fairs Cities Cup in

Kenny Watson demonstrates the kind of powerhouse shooting he is so good at . . . but he was one of the players Greig missed against West German aces Cologne in the European Cup quarter final

1967,' he recalled to me, 'and we spent the night chasing the Rangers players while their supporters sang for the whole ninety minutes. It is something I shall always remember. We lost 3-0 and were never able to match the Scots. Now I want to wipe out that memory by getting a result here. All the time in this game we shall look for a goal. We shall not play as dangerously as Rangers did in Cologne. They were too defensive and they should have lost more than one goal. We shall attack more and I think that we can do it. If we don't then Rangers, I think, can go on to become the champions of Europe.'

So that was the build-up ... yet, it was to be forty-eight hours more before the teams had their European Cup showdown. Freak snow falls left Ibrox under six inches of snow and the game was postponed for twenty-four hours. Then a squad of workmen cleared the terracings and the pitch and the tie took place in front of Rangers' third successive sell out for their European matches. Yet it was a night of gloom for all these fans, a night when it all went wrong for the Scottish champions, a night when Europe turned sour for Greig and his players.

The tie became a tale of two centres — one, Derek Johnstone who missed the first leg and did not play until the second half at Ibrox ... and two, Dieter Muller, who listened to Weisweiller's warnings, responded superbly and scored a goal in each game. Yes, Cologne did get the goal their wily old coach had wanted, and it was Muller who grabbed it just two minutes after half time. Kanopka drove a free kick low and hard into the Rangers penalty box. Flohe, so influential on the night, dummied the ball and his subtle move left Rangers' defence in shreds.

Muller read the move, though, and arrived at the far post to push the ball wide of the despairing Peter McCloy. That was the signal for Johnstone to appear, but it was all too late for the Scots. Three minutes from the end the quick-wittedness of Tommy McLean caught out the normally disciplined Germans. As they fussed over their line-up after Rangers had been given a free kick a couple of yards outside the penalty box, McLean stepped up and floated the ball over the defence and past the startled Harold Schumacher in goal. It gave Rangers a draw, saved face for them in the toughest tournament of them all, but was not enough to sustain their Munich dreams. So they went out with two epic wins to help re-build their European reputation, and with the knowledge that few teams could boast of beating such fearsome opposition as the champions of Italy and Holland in the one season!

As Greig pointed out:'Whoever wins the European Cup this season will have us to thank a little for their success because we were able to beat Juventus and PSV Eindhoven, two of the best teams in the tournament. Cologne played very well against us and I am not making any excuses. Things just didn't go right for us.'

Cologne drew Nottingham Forest, the eventual winners, in the semi-finals and went out by the odd goal after a superb game in Nottingham against Brian Clough's English champions.

But Greig had achieved something in his three games. He had wanted Rangers to re-establish themselves in Continental football. They could not have done that more spectacularly. Europe had been forced to sit up and take notice of the Scottish champions again. That was something Greig had wanted ... winning the tournament would have to wait!

THE FIRST TROPHY
FOR THE NEW BOSS

It wasn't the most glamorous beginning, against Second Division Albion Rovers, but it was the game that set John Greig on the road towards the first trophy to be decided in his first season as manager. And it was a long haul through before Greig finally held the League Cup at Hampden . . . including two tough games against St Mirren, a dramatic extra time win over Celtic, and the Hampden fight back against Aberdeen which clinched the Cup.

But all thoughts of glamour were a long way off when six thousand people scattered themselves around Ibrox for the opening tie against little Rovers from Coatbridge. Yet they did see a decisive victory as Rangers built up a three goal lead to take with them to Cliftonhill for the second leg. Two headed goals from Derek Parlane and Derek Johnstone and another shot from Gordon Smith late in the game meant Rangers would not have to worry too much about the return. Indeed the following week, on the bumpy and difficult Coatbridge pitch, Greig had reason to be thankful for that lead. Rangers could not hit form. They struggled, had midfield general Alex MacDonald ordered off and won by the only goal of the game which was scored by Derek Parlane. What mattered most though was that Rangers were through and the League Cup remained in their sights.

What Rangers wanted most now was a tie which would bring some excitement into the competition, a clash with another Premier League outfit perhaps, where the atmosphere of the Cup would grip them. Alas, it wasn't to be. Instead they were drawn against Forfar Athletic, another team from the Second Division, and a team who had held them to a Hampden draw over ninety minutes in the previous season's tournament. That had been the shock of the season with Rangers powering through to victory in extra time ... but coming so desperately close to defeat. Now little Forfar returned to Glasgow, to Ibrox this time, with plans laid for a draw. Then, they reasoned, they could take Rangers back to their own tiny Station Park and get their revenge for the previous year. But Rangers had had their warning. They remembered how difficult it had been to play against the well-organized Forfar side at Hampden ... and they made up their minds that they would take no chances. In fact, they repeated their first round win over Albion Rovers, a competent 3-0 victory with the goals coming from Davie Cooper, Tommy McLean and Gordon Smith. Four days later at Forfar the wee team from the lower leagues didn't get on any better! They did score a goal through skipper Alex Rae but by then Rangers were in control and with goals from MacDonald, Cooper and two from Smith they showed the sparkle which had won them the 'treble' in the previous season. The resounding 7-1 aggregate was a warning to any club who felt that they would surrender their trophies easily.

That was one warning to the rest of Scotland. An even more important one was given in the next round, in the game which John Greig looked back upon with pride after the Cup had been won. It was against St Mirren, the bright young boys of the Premier League, the team which had been so exciting to watch under Alex Ferguson's managership and was now being bossed by former Saints player and Southampton coach Jim Clunie. They had some of the finest players in the country including striker Frank McGarvey, later sold to Liverpool, and midfield man Tony Fitzpatrick.

And if anyone in the eighteen thousand crowd at Ibrox for the first leg wondered if these players would worry Rangers they were given their answer. In thirty-five minutes and then again five minutes after half time Tony Fitzpatrick scored as Rangers fought to contain the St Mirren attacks. They looked out of the Cup, two goals down and time ticking away ... and then they drew on those reserves of strength and character which so many other clubs cannot match. Greig made a double substitution, taking off Tommy McLean and Alex MacDonald. The switch worked, Cooper scored in sixty-five minutes, Alex Miller equalised three minutes later and a minute from the end Derek Johnstone headed the winner.

Greig knew that the game was not over. He knew there was a difficult second leg to be played the following week at Paisley, but he knew, too, that his players were reaching the peak form he had demanded.

An all ticket crowd of twenty thousand packed into Love Street for the match, Saints' fans convinced that the slender one goal lead would not be enough for the Ibrox team, Rangers' fans being just as certain that their team would march on into the quarter finals. It was another tactical victory for

Forfar goalkeeper Davie McWilliams just gets to this ball as Gordon
Smith moves in with Alex Rae challenging . . . from that 3 — 0 win against
little Forfar at Ibrox in the second round of the League Cup

Forfar player manager Archie Knox is sent the wrong way by
Tommy McLean during the League Cup game at Ibrox

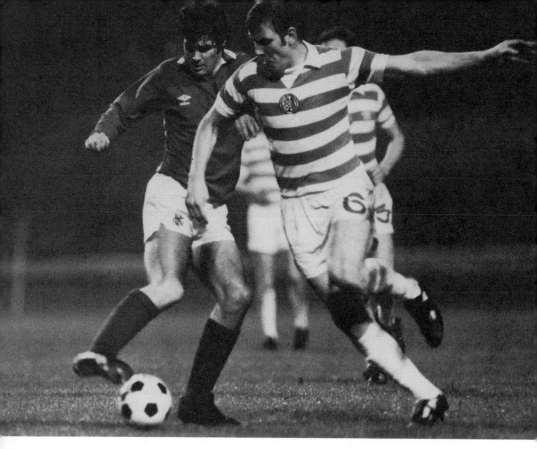

Rangers' captain hauls the ball away from Celtic defender Johannes
Edvaldsson in the dramatic League Cup semi-final at Hampden which
Rangers won in extra time

Greig who used his European look for this away game. Sandy
Jardine dropped in behind the back four to play as 'sweeper',
Alex Miller reinforced the midfield. Again the tactics worked.
Poor Saints were frustrated by that so-solid Rangers line-up,
the game ended in a 0-0 draw and Rangers were through
thanks to that amazing Ibrox fight back a week earlier.

Somehow, though, three weeks later the gloss had worn off
temporarily when Arbroath from the First Division came to
Ibrox for the first leg of the quarter final. Rangers won, but
they did not win convincingly. Indeed it was an own goal from
Arbroath centre half Billy Wells in seventy-one minutes which
sent them on to the second leg at Gayfield with a lead.

Arbroath may have been at the bottom of the First Division
but they were determined to make Rangers fight all the way.
They succeeded too. On their own pitch they went a goal down
to Gordon Smith in fifteen minutes then with a fierce wind
aiding them they hit back and John Fletcher levelled the

One of the ugly moments in the Hampden clash between Rangers and Celtic in the League Cup semi-final. Referee Hugh Alexander steps in as Derek Johnstone confronts Roddie MacDonald of Celtic. The other peacemaker is Celtic's Andy Lynch

A determined looking Derek Johnstone is foiled here by Celtic goalkeeper Roy Baines

It's Gordon Smith, almost surrounded by Celtic defenders. The men trying to stop him are Andy Lynch, left, and Johannes Edvaldsson right, with Jim Casey coming to support them

second leg score soon afterwards. Rangers battled to cling to their lead from Ibrox then and could not consolidate it until the closing minute when Bobby Russell eased the tension with a glorious shot from twenty-five yards which sailed past Arbroath goalkeeper John Lister.

The draw then paired them with their oldest rivals, Celtic, for a semi-final clash which showed the ugly side of Scottish soccer, as well as some vintage play, and once more it was a Rangers fight back which brought them glory.

It was a bitter battle between the two giants of Scottish football, one which saw two players sent off, three more booked and five goals. Celtic's Tommy Burns was ordered off in the first half for dissent and Rangers' Alex Miller after half time for a foul on John Doyle (earlier he had picked up a booking for a similar offence). The other bookings were Roy Aitkin and Doyle of Celtic.

But, the Rangers fans could forget much of the trouble. They wanted to recall the goals and the glory, the fight back which ended Celtic's bid to play in their fifteenth successive League Cup Final. They had gone behind to a Doyle goal in ten minutes, fought back to equalise with a Sandy Jardine

The ball runs loose but even the determined Alex MacDonald won't reach it as Celtic defenders Jim Casey and Johannes Edvaldsson crowd him out

penalty in twenty-six minutes and then went behind again in the second half. Tom McAdam scored that second goal for Celtic with just twenty-five minutes left. It looked like being enough until, again, Rangers drew out that little bit extra. Ten minutes from the end Colin Jackson levelled the game and carried it into extra time. In that extra half hour Rangers always looked the stronger team but the game seemed to be heading for a replay as the Ibrox team missed chances. Then they were given the kind of penalty box break which wins Cups when poor Jim Casey, the young Celtic substitute, put through his own goal.

Afterwards a relieved John Greig said:'It was hard, all Old Firm games are hard, but we deserved to win. We made more chances and we looked the stronger team the longer the game went on.'

It was a verdict shared by every Rangers fan in the near fifty thousand crowd who watched the Hampden clash ... and it pushed Rangers into a repeat of the previous season's Scottish Cup Final. For Aberdeen beat Hibs in the other semi-final and they were the opponents when the League Cup was finally settled at the end of March, after being postponed from

The goal which gave John Greig his first trophy and meant that Rangers had retained the League Cup. The ball sails past Aberdeen goalkeeper Bobby Clark with scorer Colin Jackson still in the air on the right of the picture

December because of the winter weather conditions. Fifty-four thousand trekked to Hampden for that game and they saw Rangers perform that fight back act yet again. It was their speciality for the League Cup, going behind and then battling on to victory and the Final followed the pattern to perfection!

For fifty-nine minutes the game was deadlocked and then Duncan Davidson pushed Aberdeen ahead and the Dons remained there until thirteen minutes from time. It was then that little Alex MacDonald struck with a long range shot which hit John McMaster on the way to goal and was deflected away from goalkeeper Bobby Clark and into the net. Rangers were level and Rangers were fighting for victory. They pushed forward now, scenting that the game had turned their way and when Aberdeen centre half Doug Rougvie was sent off for a foul on Derek Johnstone in eighty-four minutes, it was clear that the fates had moved towards the holders of the trophy.

Extra time looked certain as the final edged into injury time. It looked as if Aberdeen would hold out for an extra half hour — and then Rangers hit them with the killer punch. A foul out on the right gave them their chance. Dead ball expert Tommy McLean took it, flighted it into the Aberdeen penalty box and veteran Colin Jackson rose to power a header well out of Bobby Clark's reach. It was a glorious goal, a glorious winner, one which brought ecstasy to the Rangers end of Hampden. It was Rangers' tenth victory in the League Cup. But, more important, it meant that John Greig had begun his new career as manager with a Cup win.

And later he told me:'After being beaten in the European Cup by Cologne it was easy to think that if we lost this one too, then we could lose the lot. I thought some of the football was good and I was delighted to get this one under our belt to show that we are still winners. I still think back, though, to the game against St Mirren which helped to lay the foundation for this. We fought back then just as we fought back today. Rangers just don't give up ....'

Which was the lesson Alex Ferguson was pressing home to his players afterwards. 'Rangers keep playing until the game is over,' he insisted. 'My lads let their concentration go a bit but Rangers never do. They keep going until there really is no chance for them to come back. I'm disappointed because when we scored I though we could win it.'

But it was Rangers' day ... and a day for rejoicing as the Greig era kicked off with victory.

THE PREMIER LEAGUE NIGHTMARE

Rangers set out to defend their Premier League title — and the Scottish Cup and League Cup they had won the previous season — feeling they could win the 'treble' once more.

Yet if the battle for the Premier League began as a nightmare for new boss John Greig and his players, it ended as an even bigger one!

Most fans will remember the defeat from Celtic at Parkhead, the 4-2 loss which meant that Celtic were crowned champions while Rangers were left as runners-up. It is easy to recall that game with all its pulsating drama, all its changing fortunes, and say that that was the night which decided the league. It was in a very crucial sense because that night Celtic needed two points to be champions while Rangers were left with games in hand.

But it was that early season jinx which damaged Rangers, that slow start which had worried Jock Wallace in his days as manager and which returned to haunt John Greig as he started his new career. It seems unbelievable now. Many of the fans will have forgotten. But it took Rangers four games to score a Premier League goal, and another three before the reigning champions could record their first victory!

By the time the fourth game came around they had given Celtic six points lead. Look back now to that dreadful beginning, one which was salvaged for Rangers because of their European Cup form against Juventus. Twenty-six thousand fans were at Ibrox to see the League championship flag unfurled on the first day of the new season when St Mirren under their new manager Jim Clunie, were the first visitors. The Paisley youngsters obviously hadn't been told that it was a flag unfurling party for the Ibrox fans. They played well, gave Rangers problems, and with four minutes to go Robert Torrance scored a goal for them which was enough for victory. And enough, too, to mean that Rangers kicked off with a defeat!

That was gloomy enough. Worse was to follow. At Easter

In this sequence of pictures you can perhaps recapture one of the more spectacular Premier League goals scored at Ibrox last season. The man who got the goal was Rangers' captain Derek Johnstone. On the receiving end were Morton and this was one of the three goals which Rangers scored that day

(a)   Derek Johnstone bursts through on goal chased by an already despairing Morton defender . . .

(b)   Goalkeeper Dennis Connaghan is coming off his line now as Johnstone begins to play the ball . . .

(c)   Now the Rangers striker has lobbed it high into the air as Connaghan hurls himself vainly forward, hands groping desperately . . .

(d)   Connaghan is beaten now and Johnstone goes for the ball still pursued by the Morton defence. . .

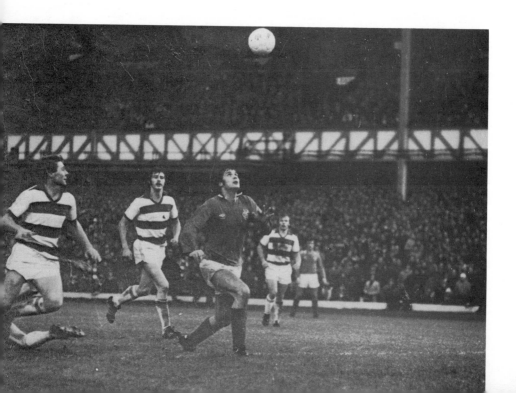

(e)   Now it's the killer touch as Johnstone dives to head the ball into the empty goal . . .

(f)   It's all over — Johnstone has scored another memorable goal and he turns to receive his team-mates' congratulations

Road the next week the champions were held to a 0-0 draw by Hibs — a foretaste of the Hibs defensive qualities which were to plague Rangers at the end of the season in the Cup Final. Another week saw another game without a goal when they could only draw 0-0 with Partick Thistle.

The following week they did score when Derek Parlane got a goal in the forty-ninth minute of their clash with Old Firm rivals Celtic at Parkhead. The only thing wrong was that the goal was a little late. By that time Rangers were trailing to a first minute goal scored by Tom McAdam and another from George McCluskey which arrived in fourteen minutes. McAdam added another before the end, Rangers missed a penalty when Peter Latchford saved Alex Miller's spot kick and suddenly Rangers were six points behind their oldest rivals!

They had gone into the game with high hopes and with specially prepared tactics. But as John Greig admitted disconsolately afterwards, 'That goal in the first minute was a killer. Our team didn't have time to settle to the formation we had worked on . . . and they never recovered from losing a goal so quickly.'

The following week it looked as if they had recovered. Returning from Turin after losing by only a single goal to Juventus, Rangers met Aberdeen at Ibrox. In thirty-eight minutes they went ahead through an Alex Forsyth penalty and they were coasting to victory, a narrow one but a deserved one. Then, the game edged into injury time, Rangers relaxed for a fatal moment and Dom Sullivan struck to equalise.

Another draw at Cappielow arrived before, finally, in their seventh Premier League match the champions scored their first win. It was a good one too. Convincingly done against Motherwell after the Fir Park team had taken a lead at Ibrox in seven minutes through Ian Clinging. Goals from Tommy McLean, Gordon Smith(2) and Derek Johnstone, though, sorted things out and at last Rangers looked title contenders!

While they had had their problems, Celtic had started to slip back a little, too. And the team which took over the leadership and remained powerful contenders until the dying days of the very long and exhausting season were Dundee United. The slick moving Tannadice team had given warning early on that they would be hard to beat. Against Rangers at Ibrox in the first clash between the two teams, an Alex MacDonald goal eight minutes from the end gave the champions a draw.

Then at Tannadice, just around the turn of the year, they beat Rangers 3-0 to set themselves on course for a first-ever

That opening game which Rangers lost, though it doesn't look that way here as St Mirren go under penalty box pressure! Goalkeeper Ally McLean punches the ball clear from Tom Forsyth with Dave Cooper, Alex MacDonald and Colin Jackson the other Rangers men in the picture

championship win. It was late in the season before Rangers could get full revenge against Jim McLean's team . . . but they started off by beating United 1-0 at Ibrox in February. Young Chris Robertson scored the only goal eight minutes from time and that carried Rangers to the top of the Premier League for the first time.

Soon, though, the fixture pile up which eventually swamped Rangers' challenge for the title, began to take its toll. Dundee United were knocked out of the Scottish Cup early and while Rangers marched on in that tournament, becoming embroiled in replays too, waited for the postponed League Cup Final and battled on in Europe, the team from Tannadice steadily picked up points. They opened up a large gap between themselves and their main challengers who had become both members of the Old Firm. When Celtic went out of the Cup too, they were given that little edge over their Glasgow rivals. While Rangers beat Dundee United at Tannadice 2-1 with first half goals

Dundee United goalkeeper Hamish McAlpine takes this one from the head of Derek Johnstone as Paul Hegarty watches anxiously

from Ally Dawson and Gordon Smith and then beat Celtic at Hampden with a goal from Alex MacDonald, the strain of playing so many games began to count against them.

When the Scottish Cup Final went to a replay plus extra time, and then to a second replay, Rangers were put under almost unbearable pressure. Yet the winning of the League was in their own hands. Indeed, it was in their grasp until six minutes from the end of that crucial Old Firm battle with Celtic at Celtic Park at the end of the season. It was a game Rangers should have won, a game they could have won . . . certainly, a game they should never have lost!

The options before them were plain. If they won they had two more matches, against Thistle and Hibs, to clinch the title. If they drew they could win it also. If they lost the title went to Celtic. In essence, Rangers had two results they could opt for, knowing that either could give them the title. Celtic had no options available to them. They had to win.

When Alex MacDonald scored in nine minutes the fifty-two thousand fans must have had visions of the title returning to Ibrox for the second successive season. Especially as Rangers clung to that lead until half time. Then in fifty-five minutes came the game's turning point.

Celtic winger John Doyle was sent off and the Parkhead team were left with only ten men and still a goal behind. That was when they raised their game, when they chased the goals they needed to take the title, the one prize left to them from the season which was ending. In sixty-six minutes Roy Aitken equalised. In seventy-four minutes George McCluskey put Celtic in front as the crowd went wild. Two minutes later Rangers had levelled things again through a goal by Bobby Russell.

For eight apparently endless minutes that's how the game remained balanced. But with six minutes left the first error came and it was Rangers who cracked, Rangers who made the mistakes which cost them the match and the Premier League title. First of all in that fateful eighty-fourth minute Colin Jackson, a hero for so much of the season, headed the ball past his own goalkeeper Peter McCloy to put Celtic in front. Then right on time it was Murdo MacLeod who scored a fourth for Celtic. They stayed on the field to celebrate while the Rangers players trudged wearily to their dressing-room knowing that yet another Cup Final clash loomed ahead of them in a week's time.

They were disappointed, bitterly disappointed, at losing that match and the championship. But they had been victims of their own success. Success in all the Cup competitions, including their run to the quarter finals of the European Cup, had taken up midweek dates which could have been used for the backlog of League fixtures. Instead the Ibrox men were left fulfilling fixtures, almost all of them vital, until the closing days of the extended season. They finished second in the League, but that was little consolation to Greig. He knew that the title had been there for his team to win in spite of all the difficulties that had been placed in front of them!

And he knew that second best was not good enough for these players. Or for himself. Or for Rangers.

The Dundee United defence are helpless as Alex MacDonald moves in to score the equalising goal during the first clash of these two teams at Ibrox last season

THE MARATHON MEN

Rangers' Scottish Cup victory last season came after the toughest campaign they had ever had to wage in the tournament's long history.

They played a total of eight hundred and seventy minutes of football before they won the Cup for the twenty-third time. As well as a replay against Kilmarnock in an early round, the Ibrox team had another replay against Partick Thistle in their Hampden semi-final, and then that epic struggle with Hibs in the Final itself. It took three games, two of them involving extra time, before the two rivals, one from Edinburgh, one from Glasgow were hauled apart.

Yet away back at the start of the Cup run, the biggest problem of all had been getting their opening tie played. The weather had started to create the havoc which brought so much chaos to the later part of the season. Ultimately they managed to play the tie against Motherwell at Ibrox just five days before the next round was due to be played.

They won through easily against a Motherwell team already bound to the foot of the Premier League. Rangers scored just before half time when Derek Johnstone slammed a shot past Stuart Rennie but after the interval Ian Clinging scored a spectacular equaliser and for a short spell Rangers had to fight.

However goals from Colin Jackson and Davie Cooper finished things off and Rangers moved on to the next round and a clash with the leaders of the First Division, Kilmarnock.

Fortunately Ibrox boss John Greig had taken a chance to see Killie in action when they played Clyde in the Cup at Shawfield. They scored five goals that night and John Bourke, their main striker, was outstanding.

Greig knew it would not be easy and little Dave Sneddon, the Killie boss, argued beforehand: 'We look on ourselves as a Premier League outfit. And all the pressure is on Rangers. They have to do something here. They have to keep the Cup after all while the tie is a nice wee bonus to us . . . .'

One of the Cup clashes which brought Rangers an unwanted replay. It's the game against Kilmarnock at Ibrox and here Derek Johnstone duels in the air with Kilmarnock's Paul Clarke

It was polite talk from Rugby Park. Nice, self-deprecating talk. But most of the Ibrox fans remembered hearing the same things the previous season when Kilmarnock put out St Mirren and Celtic in their Scottish Cup run. No one was lulled into thinking this would be an easy tie.

Indeed it wasn't . . . though again the tie was delayed. It looked as if everyone was going to be wrong when Rangers nipped in to score the opening goal of the game after only four minutes. It was Alex MacDonald who scored it after the Kilmarnock defence struggled to clear a corner from Tommy McLean. It reached the red-haired midfield man thirty yards from goal and he hammered a tremendous shot past goal-keeper Alan McCulloch. The eighteen thousand fans sat back then. They looked for more goals, looked for Rangers to turn on the style as they defended their Cup. Indeed Rangers could have scored more goals as they played delightful football for the opening spell, then they seemed to think they had done enough. And, when they relaxed, Cup fighters Killie dragged themselves back into the match. Eighteen minutes from the end their big central defender Derrick McDicken was upfield for a corner and scored the equaliser. Now Rangers were in the same position as Celtic had been a year earlier . . . they had drawn 1-1 at Celtic Park and gone to Rugby Park for a replay which they lost 1-0. The warning was there for everyone to see . . . .

Five days later the teams clashed again and another eighteen thousand fans were there to see the game. It was another torrid clash which had two players sent off in only *three* minutes . . . Colin Jackson and Killie forward Bobby Street. Rangers' Cup hero was chunky striker Billy Urquhart signed from the Highland League at the beginning of the season. he saw one header hit the bar in the first half and then four minutes before half time followed that up with one which he crashed past Killie goalkeeper Alan McCulloch. It was enough to give Rangers a win and push them into the next round. For, try as Killie might, they could not find a way through a Rangers defence in which Tom Forsyth was superb.

Now it was the quarter finals and this time another clash with a team from the top of the First Division . . . Dundee, managed by the colourful ex-Celtic star Tommy Gemmell. What's more it was another team with a new-found Cup fighting tradition. Just as Killie had shocked Celtic and St Mirren the previous season, Dundee had hammered St Mirren just the week before at Dens Park — a St Mirren team who had been fancied in several quarters as a possible Cup winning outfit!

And while Rangers prepared for the Ibrox tie by playing Cologne in West Germany, Dundee were making sure there would be no pressure on them at all. Gemmell discounted the tie as much as possible. 'My aim is promotion,' he constantly stressed. 'The Cup is OK, it can bring the fans excitement, bring the club some cash, but I have to be realistic. My job is to take Dundee back into the Premier League and that is all I'm thinking about. Anyhow we should have no chance at all. Here we are an unfashionable club taking on a team that might win the European Cup.'

Greig, though, refused to take Gemmell seriously. 'They beat St Mirren 4-1 last week,' he pointed out, 'and not many teams have been able to do that this season. I'm not going to listen to big Tam. He isn't fooling anyone here!'

In fact, the last laugh was on Gemmell. He brought his team to Ibrox hoping they could attain the form they had shown against St Mirren and hoping that Rangers might be tired after their midweek match in Cologne. It just didn't work out

Little Tommy McLean, a former Kilmarnock star, takes this ball clear of Killie full back Alan Robertson in the 1 — 1 Cup draw at Ibrox

Killie's defence is under pressure here as Derek Johnstone tries a header with team-mates Colin Jackson and Gordon Smith ready to follow up

that way. Rangers began magnificently and the game was over inside thirty-five minutes. Before the end Rangers had won 6-0 in a devastating display of attacking football and they had been just as good and just as lethal as Tommy Gemmell had said they might be!

That was the way Rangers powered into the semi-finals and a match against another Glasgow club, Partick Thistle. Another former Old Firm opponent, Bertie Auld, bossed Thistle and he had turned them into one of the Premier League's most efficient, if not most adventurous, teams.

Once more Greig felt it would be difficult. Once more he was right. And once more Rangers were burdened with an extra game they certainly did not need on their cluttered fixture list.

It was expected to be Rangers' game, expected to be a mere pause on the way to another Scottish Cup Final for the Ibrox team. That is what everyone except the most devoted Thistle followers believed. On the night at Hampden it should have turned out that way too. Five times the ball was cleared from the Thistle goal line with goalkeeper Alan Rough stranded. Twice the man who saved Thistle was Brian Whittaker, the other three times it was his full back partner Davie McKinnon. The pressure was non-stop on Thistle in the second half but it was one of those nights when Rangers just could not score. Mean while towards the end as Rangers became discouraged Bobby Houston had two openings — one he sent wide, the other he put into the net but was ruled offside. As well as the handful of goal line clearances, Billy Urquhart hit the bar and Alan Rough played superbly. It was just that kind of night . . . .

Two weeks later when room was found for the replay more than thirty-two thousand fans turned up at Hampden looking for a repeat of that first game excitement. They didn't get it. Thistle couldn't fight quite so gallantly again and Rangers did not make as many chances . . . but they did win!

The jinx which seemed to have settled on them during the first game lifted eventually, just enough to allow Derek Johnstone an opening five minutes from the end of the match. Most of the crowd were waiting for extra time as Rangers seemed doomed again not to get the goal they had tried for so desperately. Then with the minutes ticking away Tommy McLean sent over one of his perfect free kicks. Skipper Derek Johnstone was there, waiting for the ball at the far post. He headed it down for goal, Rough parried it, but back it went to the Rangers striker who rammed a shot into the net. It was not a spectacular goal but it was a vital one . . . one which carried

An earlier clash between the Cup finalists — and Rangers won this one by a single goal at Ibrox. Here little Alex MacDonald tries to carry the ball clear of Hibs' sweeper Jacky McNamara

the Ibrox men back into the Scottish Cup Final. One which gave them the chance to retain another of the three trophies they had won the year before!

But the difficulties which had followed them throughout their Cup run were barely beginning! These marathon men of Ibrox had one more long-running hurdle to surmount before Derek Johnstone was finally to hold up the Scottish Cup in triumph at Hampden.

Hibs were their opponents, of course, a Hibs team who had a Cup hoodoo of their own to beat. They had never won the Cup at Hampden — the only other time they had won it this century was in 1902 when the game was played at Parkhead.

Rangers moved into the first game as clear favourites. No one could see them lose. The bookies quoted Rangers at 4-6 while Hibs were way out at 4-1. There was, though, a fresh look about the Hibs team. Experienced manager Eddie Turnbull had grafted younger players onto his more experienced men and a great deal was expected from Gordon Rae, Colin Campbell and Ralph Callachan.

As well as these players Turnbull had the iron hard defensive double of George Stewart and Jacky McNamara at the centre of his defence and the power of Des Bremner in midfield. Also, while Rangers had their fixture list problems to contend with as they tried for the title, Hibs had only the Cup to concern them! It was a nice position to be in.

Hibs set out to make it hard for Rangers. They kept men behind the ball and although Derek Parlane hit the bar with a header they did succeed in keeping Rangers' goal chances down to a minimum and as Eddie Turnbull summed up so well afterwards: 'In the end we might have won the game but we could have lost it in the early part. But the main thing is that we know now we can match Rangers, we have come to Hampden and shown that and our young players must benefit from this experience.'

And so to the second clash — at Hampden just four days later. Hibs had learned from the first game. Their confidence had grown. But, still, their main way towards the Cup was by using solid defence as a springboard for swift counter-attacks. Rangers found it hard work once more with McNamara playing superbly for the Edinburgh men. Once again Rangers hit the bar, Davie Cooper this time with a shot just before half time. It was close. So was another of his tries which finished in the side netting. But neither was close enough and the game moved on into extra time and then dragged to another ending without a goal in sight!

It was no wonder that Rangers fans were singing a parody of one of their songs — one which went 'Bring on the Hearts, the Hibs, the Hibs, the Hibs . . .' — as the Final was scheduled for a third date, after the Home International Championship.

But this game when it arrived was worth waiting for. If the others failed to be classic Cup Finals then the second replay, with its own dose of extra time, will be remembered for years to come.

It was a game which bloomed on a Hampden pitch sodden by torrential rain. At last the two teams got it right. At last they gave the fans, those patient fans who kept returning for more, a game to savour, a final as memorable as any housed at Hampden.

Yet, at one stage, it seemed that the script was going to be tossed away, the script which had always had Rangers as obvious winners with Hibs in the supporting role. In just sixteen minutes Tony Higgins scored the opening goal of the

Hibs' right back Ally Brazil won this tackle in an Ibrox league game — but in all three Cup Finals Davie Cooper came out on top in this individual duel

game — of all three games, in fact — and Hibs took control of the Final. They were the team who bossed the game, the team who were in charge and Rangers toiled without success to change the pattern. They couldn't do it as Ally McLeod sprayed passes around and the youngsters Campbell and Rae provided problems for the Rangers defenders.

Then ten minutes after that Higgins goal John Greig sent out a message from the dug out, one which was to change the course of the match. He sent Derek Johnstone up front from his defensive position, pushing him up alongside Derek Parlane as one of two main strikers. Sandy Jardine dropped in alongside Colin Jackson as a central defender while Ally Dawson went to the right to close down on Tony Higgins.

Gradually Rangers began to find themselves and three minutes before half time they were given the break they needed — the goal break and the psychological break. A Tommy McLean shot skidded away from Jim McArthur and Johnstone was there to tap the rebound over the line. That levelled the scores and gave Rangers an edge in confidence as the teams went into the dressing-rooms.

When they came out for the second half the roles were transformed. Rangers were the team on top. They were the team who dictated how the game would be played, the team who looked Cup winners. It was sixty-one minutes before they went in front. But before that the goal had seemed inevitable. When it came it was a beauty. Sandy Jardine found Bobby Russell out on the right. The midfield man played it into the Hibs penalty box and Johnstone lashed it on the turn into the net. Hibs were down and Hibs looked out.

Rangers missed chances after that but it didn't seem to matter. Yet we should have known that this game would have another twist for us all, that this final would not allow itself to be settled so easily.

Twelve minutes from time Hibs substitute Bobby Hutchison went down in a tackle with Colin Jackson. Referee Ian Foote gave a penalty and Ally McLeod scored. Once again extra time loomed, and once again the teams were forced into that gruelling extra half hour. After fourteen minutes of it Rangers were given a penalty too but their fans groaned as Jim McArthur dived to save Alex Miller's kick.

There was a final irony to come though, the last cruel trick this final was to play on the players who had fought for so long to settle things one way or another. Rangers pressed continuously but could not break through until with ten minutes left Davie Cooper carried the ball down the wing and along the bye-line in a glorious run. He crossed and Hibs' left back Arthur Duncan, trying to clear from Gordon Smith and Derek Johnstone behind him, sent a header flying into his own net. It was a tragedy for Hibs. A tragedy for Duncan. But Rangers had deserved to win the game. It turned out to be a classic final, and Derek Johnstone was the man who climbed the steps to the VIP box at Hampden to take the Scottish Cup, his second trophy as Rangers' captain.

It was a fitting climax to the season and a glorious end to the Cup marathon Rangers had faced. Eight hundred and seventy minutes of football is a long time but it's all made a bit easier when there is a Cup at the end of it all!